LIVING ILLUSIONS

A Psychology of Belief

Michael Jacobs

First published in Great Britain 1993
Society for Promoting Christian Knowledge
Holy Trinity Church
Marylebone Road
London NW1 4DU

Living Illusions is adapted from *Towards the Fullness of Christ* by
Michael Jacobs, published by Darton, Longman and Todd in 1988.

British Library Cataloguing-in-Publication Data

A catalogue record for this book is available from the British Library

ISBN 0-281-04702-2

Typeset by Pioneer Associates, Perthshire
Printed in Great Britain by
The Cromwell Press Melksham, Wiltshire

Contents

Simple Poem

I shall make it simple so you understand.
Making it simple will make it clear for me.
When you have read it, take me by the hand
As children do, loving simplicity.

This is the simple poem I have made.
Tell me you understand. But when you do
Don't ask me in return if I have said
All that I meant, or whether it is true.

Anthony Thwaite
from *Portion for Foxes* (1977)

Preface

Rarely does an author have the chance of a second bite at the cherry when a book has already been published, unless it is with a radically revised second edition. In a sense this is what *Living Illusions* is, with its new title as well. In its first incarnation the book was scarcely noticed, and yet it received appreciative comments from many of those who read it. I received as much positive feedback as from any of my other books, albeit from what turned out to be a tiny readership. I felt it deserved more attention. I am extremely glad that Judith Longman, former Editorial Director of SPCK, felt the same way, and very grateful that she clearly believes in the book as much as I do.

When I came to revise it, I found how much I had changed my thinking in just five years. On closer analysis of my current intellectual position, I could detect that I had shifted away from the attempt at tight order and linear development to a more inclusive, networked system of ideas. This seemed to me in itself a different order of belief to that which I held at the first writing. This shift alone confirmed the necessity of such a study, and underlined my wish to adopt a significantly different approach. I doubt whether anyone will want to make detailed comparisons of the two texts, but subjectively this book has felt quite different. It has been as exciting to work on this project as the original, but the effect of the material on me has been to enlarge not just my perspective on, but also my attitude to various forms of belief.

I am grateful to my Head of Department, Bill Forster, for a sabbatical term in which to concentrate upon this fascinating area of study. My wife, Moira Walker, has been constantly supportive of me and the project, checking each chapter in draft, suggesting where clarification was needed, and encouraging me with her enthusiasm. I also wish to express my thanks to Anthony Thwaite for his generous permission to reproduce his 'Simple Poem' as the frontispiece. During this period of writing I had a brief correspondence on another matter with Ann Thwaite, in the course of which I came across the poem. I thank her for that also: it summed up immediately much that I was struggling to convey in working on the themes of illusion and belief. It appeared originally in his *Portion for Foxes* (Oxford University Press, 1977), and later in his collections *Poems 1953—1983* (Martin Secker & Warburg, 1984) and *Poems 1953—1988* (Hutchinson, 1989).

This book is dedicated to the next generation, especially to our joint family—Mary, Andrew, Susanna, Tessa and Sarah— and, first in the generation after them, Laura. These are in many ways extremely bleak times, especially for the young. If the churches are sometimes active on the social front, they are far from getting to grips with the issues that I raise in this book. Even if they did, I fear they have lost too much of their credibility to point the way whereby our children, and the next generation, might transcend (as well as cope with) the anxieties of everyday concerns: in search of, in appreciation of and in enjoyment of the finer points of life. I have no pretention or wish to supply answers, but my hope is that this book will be of value to those who ask what are to my mind some of the most difficult questions of all.

Michael Jacobs
Leicester
December 1992

PART ONE

Psychology

ONE

Illusions

———

Once upon a time (the phrase has many layers of significance) a traveller was walking alone across deserted but far from desolate country, and saw through the morning mist, on the horizon, the outline of what appeared at first to be a craggy hill. But this was far from clear. As the traveller slowly came a little nearer to the hill, its dark outline took on different shapes and meanings: at one time in the traveller's eyes it looked like a huge granite rock, which in the imagination took the form of all manner of fantastic creatures. At another point it became clearer, and it was evidently a building on a hillside. But what kind of building it might be was still not clear. Was it a castle, or was it an even more ancient monument? At this distance, the traveller could only interpret what little the eyes could see through fantasy and imagination.

As the walker got nearer, he (or she—flesh out the traveller as you will) caught up with a band of ramblers. Here was an opportunity for companionship along the way. They had a map, and several of them knew about various aspects of the landmark ahead. It was marked on the map as an old monastery, and several fellow-travellers told our walker about the style of building, the life of the order that used to live there, the lives of some of the more famous monks, the history of the decline of the order, and so on. Our traveller eagerly absorbed this information. As the group of ramblers walked, our traveller moved from fantasy and imagination to what appeared to be a clearer sense of reality, assisted partly by seeing the hill come closer, being lit more brightly; and partly by what he (or she) was told by those who knew about the place. Her eyes (or his eyes—for perhaps by now you see that he or she is Everyone and Anyone) could now make sense of the curious shapes from the silhouette on the hill. The company was pleasant. The party stopped at places

3

along the way; the traveller listened to their tales and, for a time, fell in with the customs of the group.

As they proceeded, our traveller began to feel restless. There was a certain 'know it all' quality to the companions — and, in any case, they made it clear that their route took them a mile or two away from the path to the monastery on the hill. The traveller wanted to take a closer look and so left the group to take its chosen way, setting out once more alone. As the ground rose, and the ruins came into focus, the walker realized that some of what the fellow ramblers had said was true: the architecture was indeed late gothic, and the site and layout of the building indicated that it was such and such a community. But in other respects the ramblers had some details wrong, since they had gone on what they had been told, and they appeared not to have fully explored the site for themselves. The traveller was fascinated nevertheless, and went back to the nearest village for the night; and returned the next day, seeing the building in a new light. Each time our walker approached the hill by different paths, and saw new perspectives and details on every visit. His understanding deepened, or (if you prefer) her vision broadened.

The traveller stayed for some time in the neighbourhood, and began to meet other people who also visited the hill and its ruins. At night, they talked with each other around the fire. They shared the way they saw things, and they disagreed sometimes about the factual details surrounding the place, and at other times about the way they interpreted them. But they also learned from each other, because they did not spend their time trying to convert the others to their personal view. Instead they explored the subject together, mutually helping each other by asking probing questions, all the time discovering that the place was capable of a myriad understandings. They realized that even if they stayed there for weeks, the hill and its ruins would always have new secrets to reveal.

*   *   *

'Once upon a time' — my phrase makes it clear that this is not a true story. It is not quite a fairy story, because it lacks the magic and the mystery, the romance and the revenge, although it does tell of a place viewed sequentially as magical and mysterious, which people fell in love with. Neither is it full enough to be an allegory, although its theme is the same as many such tales: Bunyan's *Pilgrim's Progress*, Homer's *Odyssey*, or Virgil's *Aeneid*. My analogy (for such it is) has neither the power nor the significance of the anonymous, mythical, symbolic or historical journeys (again choose which you prefer) of the Babylonian Gilgamesh, the Hebrew Abraham, the Israelite Moses and his people, the journey of Jesus to Jerusalem, or Paul's Mediterranean travels ending in Rome. There can also be no comparison to the Buddhist 'Way of Enlightenment', nor to the more physical journeys of pilgrimage, by Jews and Christians to Jerusalem, by Muslims to Mecca, by Hindus to Benares, by Sikhs to Amritsar. My story scarcely matches the secular equivalents which have similar mythic qualities, such as Columbus's search for the Indies (and the fascination of so many explorers' tales), the Great Trek, wagon trains and the Wild West — even novels such as *Kidnapped, The Heart of Darkness* or their visual equivalents, the cultic road movie.

So many stories, or so much history (the line is not always clear), that to suggest an interpretation would be presumptuous. But I can interpret *my* analogy, which might be one way of illustrating the journey of perception, construction and belief, because in this book I describe (with, as I shall acknowledge, all the limitations that words ultimately have) a process of development: a psychology of belief. The traveller's perception of the distant hill illustrates how early views of the world, of the spiritual realm and of the gods are idiosyncratic, fantastic, and mythical; how in the course of childhood, adolescence and young adulthood we absorb from our parents, from our culture, from our education and from religious groups (the fellow ramblers) information which at the time seems factual and historical, statistical and scientific, comfortably solid and reliable (although later the same information may be interpreted differently, as speculative and philosophical). This learning helps to ground belief, whether it be in a religious faith, in a structure of society or in an intellectual discipline. Such grounding might be understood in different ways. At first, the groups in which we move and to which we belong help root beliefs and ideas in definite and definitive thinking, through communicating their tradition; but some of these groups have the effect of grounding these

ways of construing the world of ideas and of faith so firmly
that people cannot make their ascent towards more flexible
ways of thinking, or find the richness of what I hesitantly call
'the transcendent'. The danger of such limited thinking may
be illustrated when I use this term 'the transcendent': many
readers will immediately interpret the word as meaning 'God'.
Half of such readers will feel more at ease by making this
translation, and the other half will be suspicious that they are
being fed a disguised form of religion. The reason I even
hesitate to use this word is precisely because I do not want it,
or any such words, to be limited to one narrow meaning.
Indeed if this particular word is limited it ceases to portray
the meaning for which it was intended.

There is another danger in belonging to a group holding a
common belief. All groups possess a dynamic of their own,
which is nothing to do with their particular philosophy, belief
or *raison d'être*. It is this dynamic itself which seduces and
unconsciously manipulates its members into a group faith or
group consciousness, and does not always make room for the
development of the individuals who share common ideals.
Groups can help people grow, but they can also hold people
back. There comes the time when, like our traveller, some
people feel the need to break away from their base group, to
find for themselves an identity of their own: to wrestle with a
faith, philosophy or understanding which speaks to their
experience, and not just to that of former generations or of
present peers. This breaking away is known by various
names: religious symbols include the wilderness, the desert,
the exile—although these terms might be used in exactly the
same sense as for those who have to leave other more secular
settings, disciplines, or societies at a crucial time for their
own development, and for their relationship with former
allegiances.

Our traveller breaks away, to learn for himself (or herself—
there may or may not be differences here, since women tend
to be more connected to each other than men are). Later the
traveller meets others who have done the same, just as others
often return from the desert or from exile when the greater
part of the struggle for freedom within themselves has been
won. But they do not always return the same people, or to the
same people. They often look for others, who are glad for
them to share in the quest: people from whom they can learn

in new ways — contributing to each other, receiving from each other, but no longer wanting to force themselves (or anyone else) into group norms, group rules or group beliefs. Indeed, these are sometimes the very people who challenge the rigidity of such systems elsewhere.

But the analogy can be understood in another way. It also traces one aspect of life development in which we move constantly between perceiving and making constructions of experience for ourselves, and construing and perceiving through and with the help of others. In fact, there is a link between the journey of belief and the life journey as a whole, although it is not as precise as my parallel might suggest. In later chapters, I spell out in more detail how a tiny baby, although apparently an individual, is bound up subconsciously in a relationship between self and an 'other', who is not at first experienced as a separate person. First perceptions are highly idiosyncratic, little informed by awareness of wider reality and interpreted in all manner of fantastic ways. During early infancy, a child starts to attain independence, but at the same time begins to make sense of experience through what others say, as well as through her own perceptions. From the individuality of early childhood, she moves into relationships with other children and with adults, learning from them and fitting in with their conventions and customs. This is partly because it feels more secure to 'belong' than to be 'separate' and partly because that is the way to get on in the world. Although adolescence is commonly thought of as the time for independence, in fact this is limited, and where it happens is usually confined to people breaking free of their immediate family. Those who *actually* break from conventional norms and ideas tend to do this somewhat later in life; often following a crisis. They begin a journey of inner discovery for themselves. This is again a time for individuality: it resembles the working out of personal identity (in terms of gender, work and purpose) that starts with adolescence and goes through into adult life. Although some such people choose to remain isolated, to work out ideas on their own, others continue their exploration by seeking out the company of others who are engaged in a similar quest. These intellectual or spiritual companions are valued, not because of any clear answers they may give to questions, nor for any security that might come from holding common opinions, but because they provide different perspectives towards their shared goal. At this level of thinking and believing, awareness grows that the search for total understanding is, in more than one sense, beyond them all.

'Once upon a time'—even the analogy cannot be fixed forever. At one time it means one thing; at another I understand it otherwise. When I first ventured the ideas in this book, I construed the development of belief as similar to other aspects of psycho-social development, even if it were paced differently.[1] Perhaps I also see psycho-social development slightly differently these days, but I *am* clearer now about the weakness in my analogy, because a psychology of belief is not as linear as the metaphor of 'the journey' suggests. I shall spell this out later too but, for the moment, notice again how the analogy fails (not surprisingly), and has to point beyond itself. In one sense, it is an illusion which helps a little, but which may trap us into thinking it is true. Such are the layers of 'Once upon a time', a phrase which tells us that the story is both true and not true.[2] This is the struggle the reader and I will have throughout this book: to know what might be true (as reality), what might be true (as illusion) and what might be false. My own understanding is that this dialectic applies to a psychology of belief. Perhaps this gives us the courage to see whether it might not also apply to belief itself.

Illusion—a negative view

To consider using the term illusion in the same context as belief may seem foolish. It risks raising ghosts of intellectual battles long since fought. Freud's broadside fired at religion in *The Future of an Illusion* provides an immediate and unfortunate association to the term.[3] He considers the status of religious propositions and, like the logical positivist philosophers, he argues that they cannot be authenticated in the same ways as many other propositions. He is rightly critical of the authority, appropriated by the Church at times, that people *must* believe because the Church knows right. It is interesting that Freud also draws upon the 'Once upon a time' of the fairy story as a parallel to the 'as if' quality of the religious story or proposition. He treats this theme with less sympathy however, because he cites one of his sons as a child who turned with disdain from any story that was not true: 'We may expect that people will soon behave in the same way towards the fairy tales of religion'.[4]

Freud is more interesting when he is not sniping in this way, but asking why it is that people hold beliefs, in spite of their lack of authentication, and 'where the inner force of those doctrines lies and to what it is that they owe their efficacy'.[5] The answer, spelled out in Chapter 6 of his extended essay, is that religious ideas, 'given out as teachings, are not precipitates of experience or end-results of thinking: they are illusions, fulfilments of the oldest, strongest and most urgent wishes of mankind'.[6] By 'illusion', Freud does not necessarily mean an error: mistaken ideas are not illusions in themselves. An illusion is when an idea is intimately linked to a wish: 'We call a belief an illusion when a wish-fulfilment is a prominent factor in its motivation, and in doing so we disregard its relations to reality, just as the illusion itself sets no store by verification'. Religious ideas cannot be proved, but neither can they be refuted. In one sense, Freud would not have anyone forced to disbelieve, any more than he would have them forced to believe. He tries hard to stay with his definition of 'belief as illusion' without commenting on whether it is 'good' or 'bad'. But he cannot suppress for long his intellectual conviction that religion is also in error, and his suggestion of the neutral status of illusion soon gives way to pejorative sentiments:

> Philosophers stretch the meaning of words until they retain scarcely anything of their original sense. They give the name of 'God' to some vague abstraction which they have created for themselves; having done so they can pose before all the worlds as deists, as believers in God, and they can even boast that they have recognized a higher, purer concept of God, notwithstanding that their God is now nothing more than an insubstantial shadow and no longer the mighty personality of religious doctrines.

Such a tone may win some allies, but it does little to encourage enemies to consider his central position: the concept of illusion as ideas and beliefs which incorporate strong personal wishes. In other words, illusions meet a need and express a psychological position (as becomes clearer when stated more positively later).

There is another reason for taking Freud's position seriously, despite his fierce attack on religious belief (and, it has to be said, a justifiably bitter attack upon the way religion has been used as a means of social oppression). Later in his essay, he supposes his critic objecting that his 'endeavours come down to an attempt to replace a proved and emotionally valuable illusion [religion] by another one, which is unproved and without emotional value'. Freud's reply is typical of his scepticism, which he could apply to himself as much as to the objects of his enquiry.

> You will not find me inaccessible to your criticism. I know how difficult it is to avoid illusions; perhaps the hopes I have confessed to are of an illusory nature too. But I hold fast to one distinction. Apart from the fact that no penalty is imposed for not sharing them, my illusions are not, like religious ones, incapable of correction. They have not the character of a delusion. If experience should show . . . that we have been mistaken, we will give up our expectations.[7]

Freud again shows some confusion here between illusion and error: he is prepared to concede that psychoanalysis might need to correct false thinking, but does not acknowledge that even when it is 'correct' it is *still* an illusion. But what he shows signs of doing here is extending the concept of illusion beyond religion, and beyond the other examples he gives of personal and large group illusions, to his own discipline and (by implication) to other intellectual disciplines. People *believe* in psychoanalysis; or people *believe* in particular scientific theories. It is not just a question of academic proof. There has been (and, by implication, there still is) this sense of illusory thinking throughout the development of psychoanalysis, just as there is in every intellectual discipline. There is nothing wrong with this, although analysts (in common with thinkers from many other disciplines) have tried at times to persuade each other as well as outside critics with all the language and behaviour of witch-hunters. There are, however, few 'pots that can call the kettles black' in the intellectual life. What I refer to here, and will return to in subsequent chapters, is that most of our thinking about the 'the riddles of the universe',[8] just as much as our thinking and beliefs about the riddles of humankind, can be seen as taking place on different levels: the magical and the mythical, the literal and the metaphorical.

There is no reason why religious belief should be exempt from this phenomenon, any more so than scientific theories or other intellectual endeavours. Since any or all of these levels are ways of making sense of experience, and are invested with emotional as well as cognitive commitment, it is not far-fetched to take Freud's term, to divest it of its most negative connotations, and to explore the positive side of 'living illusions'.

Illusion — a positive view

Fortunately the deeply respected, much quoted and much loved British psychoanalyst D. W. Winnicott does just this. He writes frequently about the importance of illusion and refers to 'its positive value'.[9] He explicitly relates illusion to infancy, but also to art and religion, making his thinking of special interest to this study. His positive use of the concept of illusion needs to be understood correctly if this study of a psychology of belief is to make any sense at all.

Winnicott spent many hours observing mothers and babies. He writes of a period of life when, for the baby at least, there are no words (and no adult concepts) that make sense of that early experience. Winnicott must himself therefore use concepts which can only approximate to what he and others observe, and to his way of interpreting these crucial early months. Fortunately he seldom strays into highly technical language, and I hope that my summary of his ideas will be clear for the reader who is not familiar with this particular discipline.

A new baby has no memories (except perhaps of being in the womb and of birth itself), and no previous experience with which to make sense of the new state of existence outside the womb. Previously surrounded by care and protection, with all bodily needs catered for at once, the external world presents a sudden and totally new experience. The only protection from fluctuations of temperature, from the frustrations and pain of hunger and from physical discomfort is a baby's mother. Winnicott uses the term 'mother' generically, as representing any person who has the active care of the baby. He suggests the importance of this person being the same constant figure: he wrote before the recent enthusiasm by some fathers for sharing in baby care,

but I suspect that 'mother-and-father' as an equally constant
source of care is no different for our purposes than one
parent, or a foster parent, as long as the mothering is, in his
famous phrase, 'good enough'.

We have, then, a new-born baby: raw, exposed, highly
vulnerable and unable to look after herself. We have also a
world, which like Prospero's isle is 'full of noises, sounds and
sweet airs, that give delight and hurt not' and yet can terrify
as much as Prospero's magic scared those shipwrecked upon
his shores.[10] It is the mother who acts as the filter through
which the external world is allowed to impinge upon the
baby. Winnicott describes her role:

> It is especially at the start that mothers are vitally
> important, and indeed it is a mother's job to protect her
> infant from complications that cannot yet be understood
> by the infant, and to go on steadily providing the simplified
> bit of the world which the infant, through her, comes to
> know. *Only on such a foundation can objectivity or a
> scientific attitude be built.* [my italics][11]

T. S. Eliot's famous phrase, 'human kind cannot bear very
much reality',[12] makes precisely the same point—although
Winnicott sees the mother's task as gradually introducing
more and more reality to her baby. Reality is not all bad, nor
necessarily frightening except inasmuch as it is new and
unknown. 'We often hear of the very real frustrations imposed
by external reality, but less often hear of the relief and
satisfaction it affords': as he says, real milk is as good as
imaginary milk![13]

It is in connection with the breast, that feeds the baby life-
giving milk, that Winnicott first introduces the term illusion.
He believes that a baby is born with an 'idea' of the breast
(here he comes close to the Platonic Form or Idea). Perhaps
this might be more mundanely translated as the instinctual
wish to suck and feed, although Winnicott adds to this basic
(and readily acceptable) proposition a sense in which a baby
has a fantasy (before any experience) of what he calls 'the
[theoretical] first feed'.[14] Fantasy needs to be enriched by
reality if it is to become anything more, and a mother fulfils
her baby's fantasy as she offers her breast to her baby. The
theoretical first feed becomes the *actual* first feed. We must
bear in mind here that the word 'breast' stands 'for the

technique of mothering as well as the actual flesh',[15] and that the actual first feed stands for 'the early experiences of many feeds'.[16]

Equally important for our purposes, Winnicott says that a mother provides her baby with the illusion that the baby has *created* the breast, and that the breast is part of the infant: 'I want it, it arrives, I have made it happen'. It is, as it were, under 'magical control'. We understand, from other analytic writing, that the mother-baby relationship is so close that for the first few weeks of life it is difficult for a baby to know where she ends and where her mother starts. The breast, like the baby's thumb, both belongs and yet does not belong to the baby, because a baby has no sense as yet of personal boundaries or of personal space. All is one, and one is all, making pleasure and pain, satisfaction and frustration into what appear to be total experiences, with no contrast to them: total bliss, total frustration.

The reason that this illusion is important is that it gives a baby the first sense of her power and her being: 'I exist, I can make my wishes come true, I fantasize and it happens, therefore I am'. This *gradually* provides a means of coping with times of frustration, and enables a baby to move through this early period—when reality might otherwise at times be too terrifying, such as when mother is not immediately available—to the dawning realization that mother is a separate person, and that when mother is absent she will still come. What Winnicott describes here is 'good enough' mothering. Where mothering does not fulfil this function, the depth of despair is as great for a neglected child as the joy of omnipotence is for a contented child: 'I can do nothing. I have no power. There is no hope. I cannot look after myself. Nothing happens as I want it'. Despair in later childhood and adult life is only one consequence of such experience; megalomania, in the form of grandiose thinking, *delusions* of omnipotence, and persecutory power of others might be others.

In later chapters I refer in places to ways in which belief systems can go wrong. Clearly in the neglected baby there is little basis for faith or hope in the world, since mothering provides little response either to the baby's needs or fantasies. Generally, however, I concentrate upon the constructive and supportive results of different expressions of belief, and I continue here to examine the positive value of illusion in that vein. The illusion that a good enough mother provides for her baby lays the foundation for the first moves towards self-confidence (faith in oneself). 'I *am* and I *can*.' Part of this confidence is in the ability to be creative: 'I want the breast, the breast appears, I have created it'.

This type of 'thinking' is a baby's privilege. 'The infant is not challenged at first, does not have to decide, can be allowed to claim something that is borderline that it is at one and the same time self-created and perceived, or accepted from the world'.[17] In another context, Winnicott puts it slightly differently:

Of the transitional object it can be said that it is a matter of agreement between us and the baby that we will never ask the question 'Did you conceive of this or was it presented to you from without?' The important point is that no decision on this point is expected. The question is not to be formulated.[18]

It is this same attitude to illusion that I hope the reader might hold on to, as I explore ways of understanding a psychology of belief. In later chapters, I describe the different forms which an illusion might take, but I deliberately do not ask whether the illusion fits with external reality (except in the case of what I consider to be repressive and destructive beliefs). It may or may not: for much of the time, and in many matters concerning both the intellect and the heart (thinking and belief) we can never know what reality is. Unfortunately, in some stages of faith development (and intellectual development) people have the illusion that they do know what reality is—which makes it impossible at such points, and over such issues, to think more deeply about these fascinating questions.

As Winnicott points out, the thinking that is here being described as taking place naturally in a baby, in later life and in an adult, might be seen as mad. However, he further states that:

In religion and in the arts, we see the claim socialized, so that the individual is not called mad and can enjoy in the exercise of religion or the practice and appreciation of the arts the rest that human beings need from absolute and never-failing discrimination between fact and fantasy.[19]

Similarly, Freud suggests that artists are the most successful in giving expression to both what he calls 'the pleasure principle' and 'the reality principle', which, if not quite the same as Winnicott's illusion and reality, are closely linked. However, as we have already seen, Freud is not so complimentary about religion, which he feels tries unsuccessfully to overcome the pleasure principle. To his mind, scientific thought is more in touch with reality, giving pleasure in the process of discovery, and he sees education as developing reality thinking. But despite his own scientific ambitions, Freud favours the artist as 'making use of special gifts to mould his phantasies into truths of a new kind, which are valued by men as precious reflections of reality'.[20]

What Winnicott suggests (and he admits that we do not yet *know* how far this is true) is that the world is created anew by every new baby, who starts on that task from birth, and at the 'theoretical first feed'. The way this world is created depends upon the quality and timing of the mothering. The mother acts as a transitional object, enabling the baby to accommodate subjective awareness and increasing exposure to external reality. In time, she introduces her baby to other objects, which become similar 'transitional objects' (another of the phrases for which Winnicott will always be remembered) such as a cuddly toy, a soft blanket, a smelly piece of muslin, or a dummy. These serve a similar purpose to the illusion that the mother helped to create at the first feed. It is not difficult to see how such objects help to *wean* a child from mother's breast, and from the need for mother's constant presence. But Winnicott uses an additional term here, which is also relevant to the study of illusion. Just as the mother has helped create an illusion in the first place, her 'main task [next to providing the opportunity for illusion] is disillusionment'.

Thus far, although Freud pays little attention to the detail of the relationship between mother and baby, there appears little difference between these two views about illusion. Freud criticizes religion as the failure to give up childish fantasies, and therefore encouraging a perpetuation of age-inappropriate illusions being taken into adolescence and adult life. Winnicott also shows how important it is for a mother to help her baby to experience disillusionment, when the illusion is no longer necessary, and external reality can be encountered more directly, 'face to face'.[21] The difference between Freud and Winnicott (which is an essential one for understanding the living illusions of faith, fantasy and thought that I examine in this book) is that Winnicott does not hold that illusions in adult life are to be viewed negatively. While he writes about the need for a mother to help her baby give up the illusion of creating the breast (and indeed, because of the mother-baby symbiosis, to give up also the illusion of *possessing* the breast), this is only the first of an ongoing series of illusions and disillusionments. The task of weaning 'continues as one of the tasks of parents and educators'. Again, this may seem like Freud's recognition of the importance of education for reality thinking; but Winnicott goes on:

> In other words, this matter of illusion is one which belongs inherently to human beings and which no individual finally solves for himself or herself, although a *theoretical* understanding of it may provide a *theoretical* solution . . . It is assumed here that the task of reality-acceptance is never completed, that no human being is free from the strain of relating inner and outer reality, and that relief from this strain is provided by an intermediate area of experience which is not challenged (arts, religion, etc.).[22]

I look specifically in Chapter 5 at this intermediate area as an area of play, and at the transitional space which art and religion (and, I believe, science) provide between the external and the internal, between 'reality' and 'the transcendent'. But the theme of illusion as an intermediate area is one that runs through all these chapters, with their examples illustrating different perspectives and forms of belief. Whatever point we choose to focus on in faith development and in the psychology of belief (whether it is a religious or any other way of thinking) 'we see through a glass, darkly'.[23] Illusion is a way of constructing experience, and of relating to reality, as well as to the inner world; it is an intermediate area which protects, permeates and filters, contacts, translates, and prepares us for change, as we shift from disillusion at one way of constructing reality into the illusion necessary for a new one. As Winnicott writes towards the end of the paper which so informs our thinking on illusion, 'transitional phenomena are healthy and universal'.[24] Elsewhere he puts it more prosaically, where he imagines what a healthy baby might grow up to say: 'I know that there is no direct contact between external reality and myself, only an illusion of contact, a midway phenomenon that works very well for me when I am not tired'.[25]

The significance of illusion

The idea of 'religion as projection' has been challenged by many thinkers, but it is the idea that religion is *merely* projection that is the most interesting qualification of Freud's concept of illusion. Jung has no problem with the view that the God-image might be created by men and women: 'The scientific approach makes the divine figure, which faith posits as being the supreme certainty, into a variable and hardly definable quantity, although it cannot cast doubt on its actuality in the psychological sense'.[26] In the Netherlands discussion of religion as projection has been 'at a level and with an originality which was not equalled abroad'.[27] One writer has affirmed the hypothesis of projection, but has broadened it: 'Projection is not pathological, but normal. Everyone projects, always and necessarily'. Other Dutch authors have denied the Freudian version of illusion and called it variously 'a necessary, although inadequate, temporary organizing and stabilizing system of whole perceived worlds'; and 'neither primitive, delusory nor infantile, but normal and fundamental. It is a reality *sui generis*' [of its own kind].

An American psychoanalyst, Ana-Maria Rizzuto, has also challenged the traditional Freudian view. She has been influenced by Winnicott's thinking. Not only does she criticize Freud's denial of the place of mothers, grandparents, and siblings in the emotional influences upon belief — without disputing that ideas about God are acquired early in life, she demonstrates that agnostics and atheists have also had ideas about God, and that though they hold very different views now from believers, their attitudes too are connected to the 'constraints and opportunities' of any one person's life. Building on Winnicott's ideas of transitional objects and transitional phenomena, she writes:

> Men cannot be men without illusions. The type of illusion we select — science, religion or something else — reveals our

personal history: the transitional space each of us has created between his objects and himself to find a 'resting place' to live in.[28]

It is the nature of human beings to play with toys, games, words and ideas. Many theories are attempts to assemble facts in a way which makes the puzzles they present look less impenetrable. In some senses, they are an illusion.

Rizzuto points out that Freud does the same himself, particularly when he turns his attention to anthropology and religion — he moves into 'rumination', often himself recognizing the nature of his views, as experiments, and as playing with ideas. Those who have not read Freud often fail to recognize how much he writes of his suggestions as tentative, although in some cases (such as the Death drive) he soon turns speculation into apparent fact.[29] Rizzuto suggests that such were Freud's own 'illusions', although as we have already seen Freud acknowledges this himself. As Coles suggests, since Freud describes some of his ideas about the structure of personality as 'metapsychology' and not as 'psychology', he is acknowledging their status, which makes them as distinct from psychology as metaphysical philosophy and theology is from physics.[30] The difficulty with Rizzuto's position is that at times she forgets (as Freud does) that true illusion, in the sense Winnicott and she (elsewhere) wish to use it, has nothing to do with the possibility or absence of error. Neither are illusion and reality the same; nor are they contradictions: using the term illusion in this psychological sense, essentially means understanding it as the use of objects, fantasies, words and ideas, as a way of mediating and interpreting the realities which we can never fully either know or understand.

There are others to whom I might also allude, who support the positive value of illusion. Some of them are French thinkers who can be difficult to read, even in translation, with concepts that are not easy to understand unless the reader has a particular interest in linguistics, philosophy and the theoretical end of psychoanalysis. Writers such as Lacan, Derrida or Foucault make immense contributions, although they remain largely inaccessible to most readers. Nevertheless, we can catch glimpses of their thinking, which encourages the value that might be placed upon illusion. When Lacan asks: 'Why is language most efficacious when it says one thing through saying another?', he demonstrates not only the power of metaphor, but of language generally. Potent examples are 'the pun' (which makes two statements at once, and sometimes a third by juxtaposing the original two) and 'the signifier' (the word or symbol which does not always have to point beyond itself to have meaning — it has meaning in itself). Foucault, himself partially influenced by Lacan, finds value in the concept of the unconscious as the limiting factor of all human sciences, causing perpetual suspicion of their constructions of humankind. In another's words, his view is that 'camped amongst the Sciences of Man like the Trojan Horse, [psychoanalysis] comes to disturb the latter in their anthropological sleep'.[31] Such brief references perhaps provide some confirmation for the concept of illusion extending beyond religion to all expressions of human thought. They furnish further support for a view of images, symbols and words as validly expressing meaning in themselves and beyond themselves. Such writers also warn me that, at the beginning of this study of illusion and belief, even the words I use in an attempt to master ideas, and to explain the phenomena, are in some sense illusory: 'Meaning is the fact that the human being is not master of this primordial, primitive language. He has been thrown into it . . . Here man is not master in his own house. There is something into which he integrates himself, which through its combinations already governs . . .'.[32]

Implications

Inevitably, in using models of personal development (which the next chapter reviews) and in approaching the psychology of belief in a similar way, readers may find themselves identifying with certain perspectives, positions or stages. I clarify in Chapter 2 my anxiety about using a psychology of belief to label experience, or to put ourselves or others in neat boxes. What I need to insist upon for myself (and if it is my own illusion it serves me well enough not to want yet to give it up) is that none of these illusions or ways of believing are right, and none are wrong. The nature of this paradoxical statement will become clearer in Chapters 5 and 6, and it is unnecessary for me to anticipate their content here. Such a statement may seem like the Dodo's verdict that '*Everybody* has won, and *all* must have prizes', although the idea of illusion makes a nonsense of any competition about which form of belief is the most true.[33] If the concept of illusion is to have any 'real' meaning (how impossible it is to use words without seeing how little and how much they convey!), it has to be understood as indicating that no belief is more objectively real than any other. Writing about religious experience, Jung correctly asserts that it is absolute and that it *cannot* be disputed. This is a parallel thought to my reference earlier to Winnicott's suggestion that illusion *should not* be disputed.[34] Jung goes on:

> You can only say that you have never had such an experience, whereupon your opponent will reply: 'Sorry, I have' . . . It must be a very real illusion, if you want to put it pessimistically. What is the difference between a real illusion and a healing religious experience? It is merely a difference of words.[35]

It is interesting that Winnicott has no problem with understanding the symbolism of the bread as the Body of Christ as different for the Roman Catholic community, for whom it *is* the body, and for the Protestant community for whom it is a *substitute*, a reminder. Symbols have 'at the very best a variable meaning'.[36] A Protestant may not understand a Catholic symbol, nor a Catholic a Protestant symbol; a Jew may not understand a Christian symbol, nor a Christian a Hindu one; in the faith development model that I explain in the next chapter, those who are in Stage 3 may not understand those in Stage 4, and they in turn no longer understand the appeal of Stage 3. But perhaps if nothing else, what this book might help readers in all such positions to understand is that each of these ways of believing and thinking has this in common: that each position in its own way uses transitional objects or illusions, to help those who are at such points to make sense of their experience and to interpret their personal realities. Within each belief position (there are several, as the next chapter explains), illusions can have negative as well as positive outcomes both for the person in that position, and sometimes for other people who come within their orbit. Unfortunately (for those who prefer certainties) even the attempt to determine what is positive and what is negative outcome is subjective: we judge each other through our own complex of illusions. Unless others' illusions are clearly damaging to themselves, or more especially to others, we need to allow the others to be where they are; although, as will become clear in later chapters, some belief positions are more suited to this kind of acceptance than others. This does not mean inactive acquiescence, or unlimited tolerance, because like the nursing mother, those who have a concern for and an interest in personal belief can help people find their illusions and support them in their disillusionments, as and when such times occur. In doing so, we may enable ourselves and others to move into new illusions, until such time as in turn we feel ready to give those illusions up as well, and so on, to the illusion of beyond, or (if you prefer) to the illusion beyond.

These changes may sometimes happen (in the words of Gerard Manley Hopkins), 'at a crash' as the conversion of Saul, or as 'a lingering-out sweet skill' like Augustine's.[37] But conversions can be in other directions too. Each one is a part of a journey of faith, that is likely to include unbelief as much as belief. 'Each of us,' writes Campbell, 'has a pilgrimage to make on a road which is strangely familiar, though we know we have never trodden it before'.[38] As is the case with our imaginary travellers, who (after walking all day) have met in the evening in the village inn, to share their questions and their ideas about the mediaeval site upon the hill, we discover that no two journeys are ever the same.

Notes

1. M. Jacobs, *Towards the Fullness of Christ* (London: Darton, Longman and Todd, 1988). The book is now out of print, and in any case is superseded by this reworking of those ideas.
2. 'Since it is a fairy-tale . . . the child . . . can swing back and forth in his own mind between "It's true, that's how one acts and reacts" and "It's all untrue, it's just a story".' B. Bettelheim, *The Uses of Enchantment* (London: Penguin Books, 1978), p. 31.
3. S. Freud, *The Future of an Illusion* (London: Penguin Freud Library), vol. 12.
4. Freud, *The Future of an Illusion*, p. 211.
5. Freud, *The Future of an Illusion*, p. 211.
6. Freud, *The Future of an Illusion*, pp. 212–15. The summary and following quotations are drawn from this book.

7. Freud, *The Future of an Illusion*, p. 237.
8. Freud, *The Future of an Illusion*, p. 208.
9. D. W. Winnicott, *Collected Papers: Through Paediatrics to Psycho-analysis* (London: Hogarth Press, 1975), p. 237. It is principally from his paper 'Transitional Objects and Transitional Phenomena' in that book that the unreferenced quotations in this section of the chapter come.
10. W. Shakespeare, *The Tempest*, Act 3, Scene 2: line 147.
11. Winnicott, *Collected Papers*, p. 153.
12. T. S. Eliot, 'Burnt Norton', from 'The Four Quartets'.
13. Winnicott, *Collected Papers*, p. 153.
14. D. W. Winnicott, *Human Nature* (London: Free Association Books, 1988), p. 101.
15. Winnicott, *Collected Papers*, p. 239n.
16. Winnicott, *Human Nature*, p. 106.
17. Winnicott, *Human Nature*, p. 107. I have added a comma after 'perceived' in order to make better sense of his sentence.
18. Winnicott, *Collected Papers*, pp. 239–40.
19. Winnicott, *Human Nature*, p. 107.
20. S. Freud, *Formulations of the Two Principles of Mental Functioning* (London: Penguin Freud Library), vol. 11, pp. 39–40.
21. 1 Corinthians 13. 12.
22. Winnicott, *Collected Papers*, p. 240.
23. 1 Corinthians 13. 12.
24. Winnicott, *Collected Papers*, p. 241.
25. Winnicott, *Human Nature*, p. 115.
26. C. G. Jung, *Symbols of Transformation* (London: Routledge and Kegan Paul, 1966), collected works, vol. 5, p. 62.
27. J. van Belzen, 'The Rise of Dutch Psychology of Religion', *Changes* 10:3 (1992). The following quotations in this paragraph come from this short article.
28. A. M. Rizzuto, *The Birth of the Living God* (University of Chicago Press, 1979).
29. See my discussion of Freud's awareness of all this in Jacobs, *Sigmund Freud* (London: Sage Publications, 1992), pp. 92–5.
30. R. Coles, *The Spiritual Life of Children* (London: Harper Collins, 1992), p. 21.
31. This, and the quotation from Lacan above, are both taken from J. Forrester, *The Seductions of Psychoanalysis* (Cambridge University Press, 1990), pp. 141 and 296.
32. J. Lacan, *Le Séminaire: Livre II*. Quoted in Forrester, *The Seductions of Psychoanalysis*, p. 131.
33. L. Carroll, *Alice in Wonderland* (London: Macmillan, 1907), chapter 3.
34. Winnicott, *Collected Papers*, pp. 239–40.
35. C. G. Jung, *Psychology and Religion* (London: Routledge and Kegan Paul, 1958) collected works, vol. 11, pp. 104–5.
36. Winnicott, *Collected Papers*, p. 234.
37. Gerard Manley Hopkins, 'The Wreck of the Deutschland'.
38. A. V. Campbell, *Rediscovering Pastoral Care*, rev. edn (London: Darton, Longman and Todd, 1986), pp. 82–97: 'The Journey'.

TWO

Living

Models

The models that are used to describe human development have one similarity to illusions. They are also constructions used to make sense of experience, although they are more artificial than illusions. They are different in other respects as well. Models are miniatures (although sometimes they are enlargements), and therefore they are not the real thing. They help to order realities, but we normally recognize their limitations. We do not (or at least we should not) live by them or believe in them with the same commitment that we adhere to illusions. Models are useful ways of attempting to see more clearly, since reality is normally too close for us to see the whole. They help us to step back, to look at and play with possibilities from a more objective perspective. They are usually less complex than the originals they copy and, in their relative simplicity, they present us with the illusion of control.

Life development has been described through a number of models, most of which take the form of linear progression from birth through to death. The many aspects of human growth (through infancy, childhood, adolescence and adult life) have engendered specialist areas of research. It is now possible to study the development of the body, of intelligence and thinking, of social interactions, of moral thinking and the psychology of faith — especially relevant to this book. Some of these models are relatively straightforward, and provide the possibility of outlining clear norms of development: others are much more difficult, both to analyse and standardize, because their variables and their complexities mean they cannot be fitted into neat boxes. Categories that are too well defined miss the subtleties of human development, although those that have too many qualifications and complications lose much of their value as simple models.

There are also differences in the way we can use these models. For example, if we study physical development, there are clear norms, at least at some stages of life. Obstetricians can plot the progress of a pregnancy to within a few days, and paediatricians can assess the height, weight and other physical signs and skills of a young child's development. They use these indicators to determine whether a child's growth is normal, precocious or delayed. There are norms for the development and decline of the body relating to other ages as well, such as adolescence or old age. Yet even in respect of physical development, due allowance has to be made for the variations in the speed at which individual children and young people grow, and at which every older person begins to lose some of their physical and mental abilities. Variables such as genetic inheritance, diet and standards of living (as well as certain psychological factors), mean that norms can only provide us with rough guides of average development, never with accurate information about the likely course of any one individual's life.

Research into aspects of mental and emotional development is less predictable and more controversial. It is nevertheless sufficiently objective in providing norms which may be of value in the work of educationalists and of psychologists. The development of language, of thinking and intelligence and of co-ordination have been sufficiently mapped to set certain standards. By using various kinds of test (such as those for intelligence, or observation of locomotor skills), it is possible to see how an individual child or adult relates to these standards. Most of this technical information, based upon research, direct observation and psychological tests, does not directly concern us when embarking on a psychology of belief. It does, however, illustrate the increasing difficulty of describing human growth and development, as a researcher shifts from the more quantifiable measurement of the growth and ageing of the body, passes through studies of the mental apparatus of the brain and approaches that much less precise area of psychological study: the province of Freud, Jung and other psychoanalytic writers. It is not surprising that some psychologists have disputed whether psychoanalytic studies can even be called science, since it is impossible to verify conclusions in the same way as other scientists, who can repeat experiments and test hypotheses.

While this does not render psychoanalytic studies null and void, the nature of the enquiry is different from that of monitoring brain cells. It often has more resemblance to the study of history or literature, where interpretations take the place of scientific hypotheses, and where argument over interpretations takes place on many levels. The uncovering of more factual information sometimes changes historical and literary theories, but interpretations can be radically different — even when based upon the same facts. Within the study of psychological development there are yet more specialist areas, such as moral thinking and the psychology of belief — and these become even more difficult to substantiate. Such models depend not upon measurement or statistical norms, but upon descriptive studies that illustrate shifts in thinking and perception that take place during a lifetime's development.

I have already suggested that there is much illusion about supposed knowledge and reality, and that science is no exception to this. There have been many illusions in the history of science, however much those theories were seen as reality at the time. There are no doubt many illusions still, although with more recognition of their possibility than there has been in the past. Indeed, my argument in this book is that all knowledge is to a large extent illusory: it is a way of constructing reality. But I would be foolish to argue that many of the scientific models are of the same type as psychological models.

Moreover, I shall argue that models which seek to describe a psychology of belief are different yet again from the more familiar psycho-social models from which they are derived. In most studies of human development, including that of the body, there are different norms for men and women, of different ages, and from various cultural and family backgrounds. In the study of faith development, it is impossible to lay down such norms. That is perhaps the most important qualification which the reader needs to recognize throughout this and subsequent chapters. A psychology of belief describes the different ways in which people believe and how their views evolve from one to another way of believing. It does not lay down standards which people ought to be capable of achieving. It is not a blueprint for development, as much as a model offered for playing with.

A definition of faith

Faith is one form of illusion. Again, I do not question whether the illusion itself is right or wrong, true or false. I only suggest that faith, like illusion, is an attempt to make sense of reality. It is not reality itself, however real it may feel at any one point of time; otherwise faith would not change. Faith is an example of the intermediate space in which I try to make sense of the relationship between me and my internal and external worlds. Others might want to describe this differently as 'where they fit in the universe', their place in the 'scheme of things' or as their relationship between themselves and their God. But faith or belief is a universal phenomenon, and cannot be confined to religious creeds or to spiritual experience. I may believe I am here for a purpose (and indeed different people will think they are here for a variety of purposes), or I may believe I am just an accident of the evolution of this planet. Either way, these are beliefs by which I and others make sense of our position, and which govern the way we act to a large extent.

My study refers constantly to a model developed by an American psychologist of religion, James Fowler. He has studied a particular aspect of this discipline which he calls 'faith development'. Fowler's study is about faith generally, not just about faith in religious terms, and in his attempt to arrive at a definition which is comprehensive enough to include all types of faith, he ends up with a formula which, as he says, is 'formidable in its formalism'.[1] His colleague Kohlberg's summary is rather easier to follow: 'Fowler defines faith as people's orientation to the ultimate environment in terms of what they value as being most relevant and important to their entire lives'.[2] 'Faith' includes therefore, as one of Fowler's mentors writes:

> The involvement of the Christian with God and with Christ and with the sacraments and with the moral imperatives and with the community; the involvement of the Hindu with caste and with the law of retributive justice and the *maya*-quality of this mundane world and with the vision of the final liberation; the involvement of the Buddhist with the image of the Buddha and with the moral law and with an institutionalized moral order and with the dream of a further shore beyond this sea of sorrow; the involvement of the primitive animist with the world perceived in poetic, if bizarre, vitality and responsiveness.[3]

It is of interest to this book's theme that the word *maya* approximates most closely in meaning to the word 'illusion'.[4]

Fowler would also want this semantic debate to include 'committed adherents of an Enlightenment rationalism convened in a . . . university symposium'. In addition, I would want to add that this definition of faith applies equally to the sense of meaning, or even the inability to find meaning, in the atheist, the agnostic or the unthinking bigot. While I have to acknowledge that other belief systems (for example, the way a particular scientist understands her or his discipline) do not *necessarily* carry an emotional commitment to them, I suggest that Fowler's study of faith development also has much to inform us about other forms of illusion in the field of human knowledge.

Such a comprehensive definition of faith will no doubt offend some people, whether the fundamentalist Christian on the one side or the sceptical agnostic scientist on the other, neither of whom, I imagine, would wish to be seen as mutual bedfellows. However, a psychology of belief does not take upon itself to judge whether the content of a belief system is right or wrong. My argument is that the different forms which beliefs take, the various ways they are expressed and the psychological attitudes that accompany them, have similarities across different patterns of belief and in the different people who believe in them. There are, for example, fundamentalist Catholics, Muslims and historians; others who hold magical views about religion or about science; and there are universalist thinkers who may be poets, Protestants or politicians. These different types of belief are found in all belief systems. The forms of illusions which people hold, and by which they live their lives, are common to all types of thought.

It may be helpful to anticipate some of the conclusions of this chapter, and of chapter 6, by pointing out that a common, essential feature of the final stages of the psychological models proposed by Fowler, Jung and Kohlberg is their universal dimension. These models show that faith and reflection upon life move in the direction of an openness to learning about and learning from alternative ways of understanding, towards an integration of symbols and images from other perspectives. In a curious way, as I will eventually show, even Freud's analysis of religion arrives at a similar position. Maturity is commonly described by these authors as an enlargement of vision which embraces other ways of seeing. It involves a sense of oneness with the rest of creation, and of being part of the whole. The transcendent, by definition, is larger than any religion, or indeed than any other kind of faith.

I acknowledge that some of my readers will not 'believe' in this particular form of illusion. Their alternative form of belief, particularly where it is one that sees everything in black and white, may even make it difficult, if not impossible, for them to accept the basic premise of such a psychological study: that belief not only takes several forms, but that each of these forms is valid for the person who holds it. Only the universalist position truly accepts that particular illusion.

Fowler's faith development model

The model upon which I am now drawing is one that has been developed by James Fowler and his colleagues, in a large research project carried out since the mid-1970s.[5] He and his team conducted extended and extensive interviews with people of all ages and, from the data collected, he identified seven Stages of faith, which he numbered from 0 to 6. (I use a capital 'S' throughout the book, to distinguish Fowler's 'Stages' from other less defined uses of the word.) His work is still being critically evaluated and refined, but it already provides a basis from which to proceed with a psychology of belief. In this book I diverge from Fowler's model in three particular ways:

1. I question the usefulness of one of his Stages (*see* Chapter 6).
2. I qualify the principle of a linear model.
3. I extend his model to other forms of belief than faith itself.

I also gratefully use much of his model as a valuable way of understanding belief, and will describe the separate Stages more fully in later chapters. At this point, my intention is a simple introduction to his Stages of faith.

Fowler maintains that for a Stage to exist at all it must be distinctly different from those which precede it and those which follow. The result of this is that he identifies the seven Stages as:

0	primal faith
1	intuitive-projective faith
2	mythic-literal faith
3	synthetic-conventional faith
4	individuative-reflective faith
5	conjunctive faith
6	universalizing faith

Figure 1

In developing his model Fowler draws upon three other models of development: the model of cognitive development proposed by the Swiss psychologist, Piaget; the model of psycho-social development proposed by the Danish-American psychoanalyst, Erikson (in turn partly based on Freud's model of child development); and the model of moral development proposed by the American psychologist, Kohlberg. The difficulty about combining these three models is that two of them are related to chronological development, although the third (Kohlberg's) is not age-specific. This will become clearer by taking each of these models in turn.

Piaget and the development of thinking

Jean Piaget's studies were particularly concerned with how thinking develops with age.[6] In straightforward terms, Piaget distinguished four stages in how children think. Critics have questioned his concept of stages, and also the bias in his theory that comes from identifying the development of boys as representative of all children.[7] Piaget's work is still influential in education nonetheless, and his model was used by Goldman in the 1960s in his study of the children's thinking about religion, which I use for some of my illustrations.[8] Piaget describes levels of selecting, organizing and co-ordinating experience, which is also what faith or belief attempts to do. If we put Piaget's stages alongside Fowler's, we see some parallels. *See Figure 2.*

Despite some similarities there are major differences between the two models. Piaget's stages are related to a child's age. The first two years involve elementary patterns of dealing with external objects, of differentiating one from

Piaget	Fowler
sensori-motor intelligence	0 primal faith
intuitive thinking	1 intuitive-projective faith
	2 mythic-literal faith
concrete thinking	3 synthetic-conventional faith
abstract thinking	4 individuative-reflective faith
	5 conjunctive faith
	6 universalizing faith

Figure 2

another and of learning that they exist apart from the child's own perception of them. Although this stage is not immediately relevant to faith development in adults, there is an implicit parallel between the process of differentiation in Piaget and the contrast between Fowler's Stages 0 and 1. Stage 0 is one of a pre-differentiated relationship of trust between mother and baby ('primal faith'); Stage 1 assumes differentiation to have taken place. Child analysts, such as Winnicott, also clearly observe that a child gradually differentiates him or herself from the 'breast', and learns through the processes of illusion and disillusionment the relationship between internal experience and external reality.

When this type of differentiation is insufficient in an older child or adult, it has some bearing on 'messianic' thinking, such as the megalomanic belief that seriously disturbed people sometimes have (that they are themselves God or Jesus, or some other omnipotent figure): such 'thinking' shows deep-seated confusion between the self and the other. Rare though this extreme type of thinking (and disturbed mental state) might be, narcissistic beliefs are more common, for example in the intense concern some people have for themselves. In faith terms, this may be seen in the desire for personal salvation over and above any concern for others. This is a forerunner of the type of magical thinking which is found much more frequently in early or primitive forms of belief.

In the intuitive stage (age, two to seven years) a child tends to concentrate on one particular feature of an issue, but misses other aspects. There is only a partial solution to problems; the classic example being the question about the volume of two glass containers. A child is shown one tall container, and one shallow container, each of which can hold exactly one litre of water. Water is poured into the shallow container until it is full, and the water is then poured from the shallow container into the tall glass — which in the process again fills right to the brim. When a child is asked which holds the most water, she invariably points to the tall container — a child of this age only takes one dimension into account. Neither can children see, at this stage of cognitive development, that a partial solution might also give rise to new problems. In religious 'solutions' to questions, a child's answers may give rise to other important questions which the child cannot understand to be relevant. But then this is also true of many adults! In the expression of faith, this is a stage of fairy-tales and fantastic religion (where God, for instance, is seen as a king or larger than life character but, in the manner of a fairy story, he is set alongside dragons and other mythical creatures). Mythology is a feature of the type of explanations that accompany this stage. The links with Fowler's 'intuitive-projective' and 'mythic-literal' Stages are clear to see.

The stage of concrete thinking (age, seven to eleven years) is one that consists of a major shift to systematic thought and of the ability to hold together two or more aspects of a situation. However, it is still difficult in this type of thinking for a child to generalize or to think outside her or his own immediate experience. In religious thinking, this is a more realistic period (with God, for instance, seen as a father, much more like a human figure). Explanations of mystifying experiences are often a combination of the natural, the supernatural and the artificial. Again, there is an overlap with two of Fowler's Stages.

The final stage in Piaget's scheme consists of the ability to think hypothetically, to form propositions and to test them out in thought: not just in action. Symbolic and abstract terms can be conceptualized. One researcher calls this the 'individualistic stage'.[9] It is a type of thinking which begins at around puberty. The ability to use concepts is essential for deeper thinking about faith and belief although, from this point onwards, interpretations of faith and belief vary enormously from the conventional to the mystical, encompassing the last four Stages in Fowler's model. On the whole, natural explanations are much more readily understood, without having to have recourse to the supernatural.

Although I have used some examples of beliefs to illustrate these different stages, Piaget's basic model is much more closely related to age than Fowler's is. The criticism of Piaget's use of the term 'stages' to describe cognitive development has been on the grounds that there are too many influences on a child to make it possible to produce the same stage of development at a given age. The term 'stage' has therefore to be qualified so that it allows room for the fact that children pass through the sequence of stages at different rates. It is also important to recognize that earlier stages of thinking are not altogether lost as a child moves into the next developmental stage. We take intuitive and concrete thinking with us, as we develop the capacity for abstract thinking.

It has similarly been suggested that 'the entire religious development of the child has a much slower tempo than the development of any other field of his experience'.[10] Recognition of this is of the highest importance in attempting to integrate the stages of cognitive development with a psychology of belief. Religious faith, in common with philosophy, is by far the most difficult area for discourse, because it relies on abstract concepts, upon internal rather than upon external experience, and upon thinking and feeling more than upon the other senses. It is little wonder that religious thinking in many adults has not moved far beyond the intuitive or the concrete, even when in other areas of thought and experience many of these same people are able to use more abstract ideas. This slow tempo of development, in the area with which a psychology of belief is concerned, means that chronological age has little significance to this study. It is for this reason that I have not included ages alongside Piaget's stages in Figure 2, because although they may apply to his model, they do not apply to the Fowler Stages. The Fowler Stages 1 and 2 might be found in an adult as easily as they are in a child. Some of the psycho-social models I examine below are also age-specific, although I shall not use them in that way.

Kohlberg and moral development

Kohlberg's research area is the development of moral thinking, and attitudes as they influence people in their moral judgements.[11] Although this preceded Fowler's initial work on faith development, the latter's publications gave rise to further thinking by Kohlberg on the relationship between moral and faith development, and to the question of the significance of faith in moral attitudes.

Kohlberg outlines six stages of moral development, divided into three levels of judgement, each level consisting of two distinct stages. The basis of moral judgement progressing through the three levels is pre-conventional, conventional and self-accepted moral principles. The parallel between Kohlberg's and Fowler's Stages reflects that the development of moral thinking probably precedes faith development:

Kohlberg		Fowler
level of judgement	basis for moral decisions	faith development stages
(pre-conventional)	fear 1	0 primal faith
	self-interest 2	1 intuitive-projective faith
(conventional)	conformity 3	2 mythic-literal faith
	social order 4	3 synthetic-conventional faith
(self-accepted)	rights of others 5	4 individuative-reflective faith
	universal principles 6	5 conjunctive faith
	'stage 7' 7	6 universalizing faith

Figure 3

Kohlberg's first six stages can be described briefly by indicating the basis for moral thinking and action in each one, and its equivalent Stage, where religious belief is used as a basis for moral decisions. (The seventh stage is in a class of its own, hence the inverted commas.) In the first stage, the motive behind moral decisions is *fear* of superior powers such as parents, and the need to protect oneself against punishment. God, as Freud suggests, is like a super-parent, experienced by people as the author of punishment or reward. The second stage, which is also part of the pre-conventional level, involves a different, self-focused motive; in this case satisfying one's own needs through 'bargaining' with others. 'I'll scratch your back if you'll scratch mine' is Kohlberg's summary of this stage, with its religious equivalent being, 'You be good to God and he'll be good to you'.[12]

The third and fourth stages form the conventional level of moral judgement. In the third, moral decisions are based on a desire to conform to the expectations of the community and, on doing good, to gain approval and to please other people. It is a stage which coincides with children going to school and meeting the socialization process for the first time. There they come up against the rules and pressures that lead to social conformity. Religious reasoning in this stage sees God as ideally good, and the protector of goodness: common images of him (and 'him' it normally is) are as a personal deity, a friend or a caring shepherd. The fourth stage is one where decisions are made on the basis of doing one's duty, respecting authority, and of working to maintain the social order for its own sake. In psycho-social development there is an equivalent stage sometimes seen towards the end of adolescence, when young people move from dependence upon authority to respect for it, and from periods of anarchic thinking to an understanding of what society expects of them. Religious thinking linked to this fourth stage sees God as bound by his own laws, and as the ultimate ground of order. Such thinking (where it is present as a basis for this moral stage) often expresses reverence for God's order and moral law. The term 'God' may not necessarily be used, but may instead be conceptualized in even more abstract terms such as 'the supreme being' or 'the cosmic force'.

The fifth and sixth stages in Kohlberg's model comprise the third level, one where moral principles are self-accepted rather than based upon conventional rules. Stage 5 is represented by moral thinking which respects the rights of others, and which upholds society's duty not to violate the rights of the individual. Moral situations are more complex, and situations may necessitate upholding the rights of the few against the apparent good of the majority (e.g. positive discrimination). In this stage, if religious reasoning is also involved, it represents God and human beings as mutually involved in creating a community in which dignity and freedom is encouraged. The sixth stage is one of much greater orientation towards individual conscience, over and above socially ordained rules, with recognition that moral responsibility sometimes means disobeying unjust laws. It has its equivalence in Fowler's Stage 6, where he suggests (somewhat exaggeratedly, as I argue in Chapter 6) that people at this faith position sacrifice their lives in the fight against injustice.

A brief explanation is necessary of 'stage 7' on the Kohlberg side of Figure 3. Kohlberg finds it difficult to stop at the sixth stage, because he feels that some kind of religious reasoning is required to support the sixth stage of belief in principles. The question he asks of each stage is 'Why be moral?' At the first level it is self-interest which acts as the driving force. At the second level it is social pressure and the need to conform. But when the third level of self-accepted principles is reached, why be moral? The motivating force appears to involve questions about meaning. 'Ultimate moral maturity requires a mature solution to the question of the meaning of life.'[13] It is for this reason that Kohlberg suggests a somewhat imprecise 'stage 7', nearly always enclosed in inverted commas, to show that it is more a metaphor than an actual stage. Since I argue in Chapter 6 that Fowler's Stage 6, 'universalizing faith', is not a separate stage of development, I would prefer to see it placed in inverted commas too, since it seems to be a metaphor for a goal or an aim, rather than a state of faith development which people actually achieve.

Kohlberg believes that 'stage 7' arises out of the despair that comes from the realization of one's finiteness, and of the meaninglessness of the finite compared to the infinite. There is a link here to the work of the existentialist theologian Paul Tillich, whose analysis of anxiety is that it arises out of the recognition of death and despair. Tillich's description of courage (one of the 'cardinal moral virtues') is the affirmation of the power of life over death.[14] I return below to Tillich's model of stages of faith, or in his case 'world-views'.

The resolution of despair gives rise to 'stage 7'. It represents a state of mind in which there is a sense of being part of the whole of life, of being identified with a cosmic, infinite perspective. Kohlberg contrasts such a view with his stage 6 perspective, which he calls 'universal humanistic'. In religious terms, 'stage 7' is expressed as a sense of union with God, but Kohlberg (like Fowler) has a broad definition of faith, and states that it need not be of a religious order. He deliberately cites the Roman emperor Marcus Aurelius as an example of 'stage 7', although he adds a further example of a Quaker woman whose religious orientation was a blend of Eastern and Western mysticism. One of the problems of such actual examples is that 'stage 7' then ceases to be a metaphor and becomes instead a definite stage.

Another distinction about this stage is that he describes it as the only one where the style of faith (in its broadest sense) comes first. In the first six stages Kohlberg claims that attainment of a particular moral stance is necessary for the equivalent religious stage to be reached. This suggests that people do not develop a specific moral attitude out of, or because of their religious faith (as tends to be the belief of many religious people, and of politicians who want the churches to lead the moral reclamation of society). If Kohlberg is correct (or indeed only partially correct), such a hypothesis seriously questions the value of preaching and teaching that tries to promote moral change and moral action by arguing from theological ideas and images. 'God loves you, therefore love one another' makes little actual sense until a person has reached the stage of being able to love another from motives other than pure self-interest. For the development of mature attitudes in making moral judgements, we may well have to start with human relationships—as indeed Winnicott says of infancy and moral development. I explain this further in the next chapter. There is nothing new in this, since the great teachers of the different world faiths, taught through stories and parables, drawing parallels from ordinary stories about human beings, about the nature of faith, of the moral life, and the divine; for example: 'If you . . . know how to give your children what is good for them, how much more will your heavenly Father give good things to those who ask him'.[15]

If belief arises from moral attitudes, and moral attitudes develop from interpersonal relationships (starting with the mother-baby pairing), the logic might be that belief itself is closely related to personal development. This is illustrated in the next chapter, although I suspect that it is more the *content* of belief rather than the *style* or *stage* of belief that comes from interpersonal experiences (especially those in infancy and childhood). The development of belief which subsequent chapters describe is influenced by social milieu and by education. I suggest that it is life experience as an adult which is the prime motivating force for disillusionment and the replacement of outworn illusions with new ones.

It is extremely doubtful whether a psychology of belief can be separated from the growth of the whole person. For that reason, it is necessary to turn to some of the models of psycho-social development. Therefore, starting with Erikson, I complete the three major influences upon Fowler's model of faith development. But I need to go beyond Erikson, and back to his own mentor, Freud, in order to arrive at a more complete expression of a psychology of belief than Fowler alone can be expected to provide.

Erikson's Eight Ages

Building upon Freud's three stages of sexuality in childhood, together with the stages Freud identifies as latency and adolescence, Erikson has developed a more extensive model which is called 'The Eight Ages of Man'.[16] (I shall utilize a capital 'A' to differentiate Erikson's concept of 'Age' from more general uses of the word.) While the phrase 'Ages of Man' is indicative of the time when he wrote, Erikson (and Kohlberg) have been criticized on the same grounds as Piaget for assuming that the development of boys and men is also typical of girls and women. It is interesting that Freud, although he concentrates upon the psycho-sexual development of boys, in the end admits that he does not understand women, and that others would have to undertake this research.[17] Many of his followers have not been as aware of their bias as he sometimes was of his own, and some of them have imagined that their gender awareness was greater than it turns out to have been. Gilligan concludes her study of these matters *In a Different Voice* with the words:

> As we have listened for centuries to the voices of men and the theories of development that their experience informs, so we have come more recently to notice not only the silence of women but the difficulty in hearing what they say when they speak . . . The failure to see the different reality of women's lives, and to hear the differences in their voices, stems in part from the assumption that there is a single model of social experience and interpretation. By positing instead two different modes, we arrive at a more complex rendition of human experience which sees the truth of separation and attachment in the lives of women and men and recognizes how these truths are carried by different modes of language and thought.[18]

There are issues about women and men as being distinctly

different which must be considered throughout any study of psychological development, as well as in a psychology of moral development or in a psychology of belief. I return to this important area in Chapter 5. For the time being the gender limitations of all these models need to be borne in mind.

Although Fowler has been strongly influenced by Erikson's Eight Ages, and himself sets out the two models side by side, I am less sure about the value of this. Where Erikson's Ages help is not in their developmental sequence, as much as in the issues they raise for personal development, many of which, I believe, are replicated in faith development. However, they occur for the most part at completely different stages of life. The model may hold good when comparing Erikson's first Age, the oral stage, with Fowler's Stage 0 of 'primal faith', because the link of mother and baby holds true. There may also be some parallels between Fowler's Stage 5 ('conjunctive faith') and Stage 6 ('universalizing faith') and Erikson's eighth Age, where there are similar objectives of achieving integrity. These are indeed useful parallels and I shall exploit them further. But it is less clear how the intermediate Ages and Stages fit together except by taking each of Erikson's key issues, and relating them at separate points to Fowler's Stages. Thus the issues of autonomy in the second Age (the toddler) can be related to Fowler Stage 4, where a person becomes more autonomous in their belief.

I will not anticipate here the substance of following chapters, which show how Erikson and Fowler each contribute to the understanding of a psychology of belief. For the present, it is sufficient to list each of Erikson's Ages with the key developmental issue which Erikson identifies as being particularly applicable to each Age. These will be integrated later with other models. *See Figure 4.*

Each stage of life brings with it a special, developmental task, which is sometimes resolved well, and sometimes not so well. In the 'oral sensory Age', Erikson proposes that the issue which has to be worked through is one of trust in the mother and, through her, in the small world that then encompasses the baby: from this trust comes initial faith, and through such trust faith in one's own being. He also believes that it is important to learn mistrust as well, because it is not safe to trust every situation. (A sense of guilt [a third Age issue] is

Erikson: psycho-social development		
	'Age'	developmental issue
1	oral sensory	trust vs mistrust
2	anal-muscular	autonomy vs shame
3	locomotor-genital	initiative vs guilt
4	latency	industry vs inferiority
5	adolescence	identity vs role confusion
6	young adulthood	intimacy vs isolation
7	adulthood	generativity vs stagnation
8	maturity	ego integrity vs despair

Figure 4

also an important part of development, and other writers have shown how necessary a sense of guilt is in learning to care for others.[19] I examine this in Chapter 5.) This first Age lays the foundation for trust and faith in the succeeding ages of life. (Similarly, I explain in Chapter 3 how this idea is supported in other studies.)

If there is a failure in nurturing, whether accidental or deliberate, the outcome for a baby is likely to be too much mistrust and little or no ability to believe either in others or in the rudimentary self. The outcome of each Age also strengthens or weakens the facility with which a person can cope with the developmental tasks of the next. Belief in oneself, for example, is important in approaching the tasks of the 'muscular-anal' Age: physical development necessitates dealing with fresh possibilities, such as walking, taking objects apart and putting them together, or toilet training. The basic issue that has to be tackled in this Age is one of autonomy versus shame and doubt.

One of the weaknesses of Erikson's model of Eight Ages is that they appear too neatly age specific. While at first sight (especially in his original diagram) they look like an ascending staircase, one of his interpreters (Capps) makes it clear that Erikson also uses other images of development. Firstly he suggests that the different generations interlock like cog-wheels, so that movement in one generation is an integral part of movement in the next: thus adults develop as parents at the same time as their children grow through childhood. The second image that Erikson employs is that of a series of concentric circles, where the boundaries of an individual's relationships expand as life progresses, from interaction with the maternal figure, through relating to both parents, to the whole family; from school, friends and the wider peer group to close relationships outside the family, from relationships at work and in society to identification with the universal.[20] I have myself tried to combine these different images of straight ascent and the circle by showing that Erikson's model of human development can best be understood through the analogy of a spiral staircase, which has eight treads to each complete turn of its ascent.[21] The major issues in human development (the Eight Ages with their strengths and weaknesses in Figure 4) appear in some form at every stage of life (each circular flight). At the same time each of the issues forms a vertical line passing through each of the flights. Trust, for example, is not just an issue in the first Age, but takes a different form in later Ages, and has to be renegotiated as an issue throughout life. Autonomy issues are not confined to the second Age (the toddler), but appear at all Ages. It is important to recognize that each of the basic issues may arise in a new form at every other age, and that none of the issues is ever completely resolved. Furthermore, under stress an apparently achieved strength may give way to its underlying opposite.

Erikson has also suggested that each of the ages of individual development contains a factor which can be applied more universally to the development of a mature society. He relates faith and religion as part of society's structure to the oral Age, the importance of law and justice to the anal Age, the relevance of role to the genital Age, etc.[22]

Erikson shows considerable interest in religious issues and in people of faith, including two fascinating psycho-biographies about Luther and Gandhi respectively.[23] He also gives some attention to rituals in relationships and in society, as well as in religious practice, relating different rituals to the Ages of his model of human development. Thus, the *numinous* aspect of ritual is connected with the first Age, the oral stage. In sacred rites experience of the numinous includes the act of looking or being looked upon. Participating in ritual is often a very positive experience, although Erikson also looks at the

negative effect of 'ritual excess': in the case of *looking* and the
numinous the ritual excess is *idolatry*. I examine this more
fully in the next chapter.[24]

Jung

Behind Erikson stand the founders of psychoanalysis:
principally Freud, whose basic model I will address shortly.
If I appear to pass over Jung's work rather swiftly it is not
because Jung is, in greater part, quite a difficult writer to
comprehend. This may be true of much of his esoteric writing
on symbols and archetypes, where images are piled upon
images, and the reader is steeped in the richness of a hundred
and one cultural traditions. Yet Jung's model of human
development is simplicity itself: in its most basic form consisting of just two stages — the first and the second half of
life. The first half of life, up to the mid-point of thirty-five to
forty years of age, is concerned with establishing oneself,
through marriage, building a family, and developing the skills
necessary for work and a career. It is essentially an outward-
looking period. The second half of life is more concerned with
an inward journey, with understanding oneself, with finding
new meaning and purpose, and above all with the process
which Jung calls 'individuation'. This goal links well with
Erikson's eighth Age of ego integrity, and with Fowler's
Stages 5 and 6, although it is necessary to note that Jung's
idea of individuation is quite different from Fowler's Stage 4,
of 'individuative-reflective faith'. (I shall come back to this
later.) Fowler's term means becoming more ego-centred or
individualistic, whereas Jung describes a process of becoming
more aware both of our uniqueness, and of our personal
unconscious *and* the collective unconscious (the latter a
Jungian term). He also includes our relationship to 'all living
things, even with inorganic matter and the cosmos itself'.[25]
Again I shall return to these ideas in Chapters 5 and 6. In
Jung's interpretation of archetypes religious figures (such as
Christ) are symbols of wholeness and individuation.

As was the case with Erikson's scheme, we have to be
careful not to confine developmental tasks to particular
periods of life. Individuation begins before the second half of
life, and dimensions that are particularly active in the first
half of life do not cease to be relevant: work, family

relationships and sexuality, for example, all continue to play an important part in the lives of most people, despite their ageing. In fact, Fordham's description of two halves of life is a little misleading, because Jung also divides life into four stages: childhood, youth and young adulthood, mid-life and old age. Samuels' very helpful guide, to Jungian and post-Jungian thought and practice, points out that a major strength of Jung's work is that he was a 'whole of life psychologist'.[26] Samuels is himself concerned about the idea of stages of life suggesting a linear process or progression through separate stages—a necessary qualification which I have already stressed and which I shall return to again and again. 'Individuation is a life-long process, a tortuous and slippery path.'[27]

One of Jung's major contributions has been the identification of psychological types, such as intuitive, thinking, feeling, and sensing persons, and introvert and extrovert personalities. These categories are a different expression of the character types I refer to below (see Freud). Their relevance here is to a rather different approach to the study of personality, which has caught the attention of some psychologists and educators, particularly in the churches. This is the Myers-Briggs Type Indicator.[28] Unlike any of the other models I examine in this chapter, Myers-Briggs does not describe linear progression in developmental terms. Instead the paper test 'places' subjects in one of sixteen different categories of temperament. The profile is careful to avoid judging as right or wrong the many characteristics that are ascribed to the test subject. Nevertheless, an individual may be able to identify personal strengths, as well as weaker areas in the personality. Myers-Briggs is a useful tool for helping people to reflect upon themselves with a certain degree of objectivity. But it is, as it were, a snapshot of a person rather than a journal of their development. Although there are clearly introverted and extroverted ways of expressing belief, and different emphases in the way people think about, or feel or sense their faith, I regard neither Myers-Briggs nor Jung (despite his obvious interest in religious thought and imagery) as making a significantly distinctive contribution to this particular study of a psychology of belief. Neither does the Enneagram, based on Sufi ideas but also used within Christian circles, which similarly provides a sketch of the personality.[29] It may be that those who are familiar with the application of these forms of personality profile will feel able to integrate them into the more Freudian scheme, which lies at the basis of my own framework of patterns of belief.

Freud: three developmental themes

Given Freud's disparaging use of illusion to dismiss the relevance of religious belief, it may seem surprising that he can be of any positive value in formulating a psychology of belief. Furthermore, common understanding of Freud's main contribution to psychology is that it lies in the area of sexuality in childhood — again, scarcely material that might serve our immediate purpose.

Such a view provides only a caricature of Freud's thinking, which includes so much more, such as the profound importance of recognizing the power of the unconscious, and the formation of personality through the influence of childhood experience and of fantasy. Freud's theory is also capable of being understood on a number of other levels. There are hints in his own work of the limitations (as 'facts') of many of his propositions (I have already noted that he called much of his work 'metapsychology'). It is certainly the case that the majority of those who make active use of Freud's pioneering work today understand many of his ideas as metaphors — approximations that attempt to describe observations — and concepts that point beyond themselves to other aspects of similar situations. Bettelheim, for example, describes the Oedipus complex as 'a metaphor operating on many levels'.[30] It is not simply about three-person relationships, important though these are in developmental processes. The metaphor is linked to other examples of 'castration anxiety': another term that is a metaphor standing, for instance, for the loss of the breast in weaning (where mother is the third force intervening between her baby and her breast); and also for the loss of power which women experience in a society in which men intervene to prevent them from achieving the full measure of their potentiality — men tend to render women impotent. We have already seen how metaphors are also used in Winnicott's work: the 'breast' stands for the nursing mother, and 'mother' is a metaphor for the principal nurturer(s) of the baby.

In Freud's early essays on sexuality, he suggests three stages of infant development, each centred on a particular pleasure-giving (or tension-relieving) part of the body. These are called 'oral', 'anal' and 'phallic' stages. Freud also describes a period of latency (between five and twelve years) and adolescence — which is strictly speaking the genital stage, although the genital stage is also used (as in Erikson) as a term for the phallic or oedipal stage. I have explained how Erikson extends Freud's apparently narrow base, adding adult stages to his life development model, and expanding the terms 'oral', 'anal' and 'genital' to include more than the three erotogenic zones; although Freud has shown this extension of interest by including the rough and tumble of physical games and play in his description of the anal stage.[31] In his own work, as becomes clearer in the writing of those who followed through his original ideas, equal importance has to be attached to the *relationship* between a child and her or his parent(s), in which feeding, toilet training, and early expression of sexuality are means through which different aspects of the relationship are mediated.

In the oral stage, for example, the mouth is the means by which a baby makes intimate contact with her mother, and with other objects, which are often put to the lips or in the mouth as a way of exploring them and relating to them. The term 'oral' in the end becomes a symbol for the total relationship, in which a baby depends upon her mother, and builds up trust in her. We shall see the relevance of this as a foundation for faith. The anal stage is one where a child learns how to be more independent, but with increasing mobility and ability also needs to learn how to fit into family rules and conventions. Hence 'anal' stands for all kinds of issues other than toilet training, including questions of autonomy and relationships to authority. The various terms for the third stage ('genital', 'oedipal' and 'phallic') similarly stand for more than three-person relationships and incipient genitality. Competitiveness and sharing are issues which are related to this period of development. Therefore, the terms 'oral', 'anal' and 'genital' need to be understood as symbols, or as shorthand words, which also describe features of relationships to other people (with whom and to whom the bodily functions that the terms originally described are also related).

A similar extension of these terms is found in the description of 'oral', 'anal' and 'genital' characters — indeed one of Freud's colleagues, Wilhelm Reich, sets out a strong case for such 'character analysis'. But the more relevant use of these terms, in our present context, is related to the character of religion and of patterns of belief. A Dutch pastoral theologian, Heije Faber, analyses religious imagery, thinking and behaviour, using Freud's three childhood stages (together with adolescence), and arrives at descriptions of oral religion, anal religion, genital religion and adolescent religion.[32] Oral characteristics (which I prefer to call trust and dependency issues) clearly form an important part of religious faith and experience, and are especially seen in primitive religion or simple forms of religious belief. Anal characteristics (rules, authority, punishment) are equally evident, in individual expressions of faith and in legalistic religion. The area of sexuality is one with which many religions have difficulty. Faber equates adolescent religion with more radical expressions of faith. In subsequent chapters I refer to Faber's work in more detail.

A similar use of Freud's stages of psycho-sexual development, but drawing as well upon anthropological, historical and sociological research in support of Freud, is found in Badcock's study *The Psychoanalysis of Culture*.[33] His fascinating book cites evidence, the merit of which I am personally not in a position to assess, but his central model is one which has similarities from a cultural and societal perspective to Faber's work on institutional and individual religion. Badcock relates primitive animistic religion to the early stage of 'primal narcissism' (the oral stage), totemism to the oedipal stage, polytheism and monotheism to latency, Catholicism and Protestantism to adolescence and psychoanalysis to maturity.[34] Of Catholicism Badcock writes:

> In the richness and diversity of its ritual and belief no religion has ever surpassed Catholicism. The reason is clear: Catholicism contained something to gratify every aspect of man's mind. He could call on the Saints to satisfy his latent animism; he could attend the totem-feast of the Mass and gratify his Oedipal ambivalences; he could pray to the Virgin in order to sublimate his incestuous love for his mother; he could fear God the Father to gratify his

conscience. In its almost inexhaustible religious riches, Catholicism could be all things to all men.[35]

I suspect that Badcock has not given sufficient attention to other developed world faiths, in what almost amounts to eulogy in his analogy. In fact, Catholicism is not sufficient in his opinion, and he sees psychoanalysis as the culmination of cultural development 'in so far as it can be considered a stage in the evolution of religion'.[36] Even then, he believes 'that if psychoanalysis is to succeed in being the final resolution of man's neurosis, it will have to shift its main interest away from individual psychotherapy towards education and applied social psychology'.[37] I shall only make passing reference to this thesis, which betrays in the end too literal a belief in psychoanalysis for me to consider it as the last word. It is largely a historical (and pre-historical) study of belief; but Badcock's use of Freud's stages as a backbone for his work supports their use in a similar way in this study of different forms of belief.

I find the Freudian stages particularly relevant as themes which, although they appear first in infancy and childhood, weave their way throughout life. What I have already said of Erikson's model applies equally to Freud. I prefer to summarize the 'oral', 'anal' and 'genital' themes by the major issues they each represent, and it is these which form the basis for my treatment of the 'stages' of belief:

Trust and Dependency (oral)
Authority and Autonomy (anal)
Competition and Co-operation (oedipal/genital)[38]

By belief, I mean both (as in the case of Faber or Badcock) the stages of religious belief, and also belief in the even wider sense of the illusions that are relevant to different states of knowledge. In Chapters 3, 4 and 5, I show how relevant these three sets of themes are to expressions of belief, through linking sections of each of the models in this chapter.

World-views, a Metro map and faith frameworks

Having concentrated to this point on psychological studies of personal development, I conclude this collection of models with three that come from theological studies. I do so with some hesitation. I do not wish to deter those who hold a religious faith from gaining from a psychological approach to belief. Neither do I want to deter those who normally have little room for religious belief from using the benefits that might accrue from a study of theological dimensions that might .support such an approach. The three theologians, upon whom I now draw, add considerably to the argument I am making. The models that each scholar suggests are equally relevant to other faiths and to non-religious belief systems.

Paul Tillich, whose thought is perhaps better known by those who have read John Robinson's *Honest to God*,[39] understood psychoanalytic theory well from his friendship with Fromm and other neo-Freudians. Although there is no clear evidence that he draws upon it, Piaget's research into cognitive development also finds some parallels in Tillich's description of three types of world-view. A world-view is an individual's way of seeing, experiencing and understanding the world. It has some similarity to Fowler's definition of faith as 'people's evolved and evolving ways of experiencing self, others and the world'.[40] These parallels become clearer when set out in diagrammatic form:

Piaget		Fowler	Tillich
sensori-motor intelligence	0	primal faith	world-view A pre-conscious literalism
intuitive thinking	1	intuitive-projective faith	
concrete thinking	2	mythic-literal faith	world-view B conscious literalism
abstract thinking	3	synthetic-conventional faith	
	4	individuative-reflective faith	?
	5	conjunctive faith	world-view C broken myth and the use of symbols
	6	universalizing faith	

Figure 5

World-view A is a natural first stage of literalism, which is found in 'primitive' religion as well as in childhood, where the mythical is taken literally. The person who holds world-view A does not even understand what myth is, since there is no need to question in this world-view. An example of such a view would be a person who believes that, as the Bible says, God made the world in six days, which is understood as

meaning six 24-hour days. Normally, world-view A provides
a safe and secure way of understanding experience (however
grim the rest of life may be). If nothing else stays constant, at
least a person's belief remains secure and unquestionable. It
may provide a way of comprehending disaster as God's will.
Such a literal view of things is not necessarily confined to
religion: other beliefs can be held just as literally, whether it
is in a particular political system or social order, or in the
'magical' power of forms of healing. That there could be any
other way of seeing or believing is inconceivable.

However, if (or when) such a person begins to ask
questions, world-view A becomes untenable. Consciousness
has been awakened, and it cannot be put aside. The state of
innocent belief has to be left behind. The next stage tends to
be world-view B, which for some people is temporary on the
way to other views; and for others (perhaps for many) is the
stage where they stay. At such a point, for example, the six-
day Creation of the world becomes untenable because
geological and other evidence seriously questions this view-
point. People who hold world-view B turn to authorities for
answers to their new found questions, but the answers they
are given often satisfy them in a way that is almost as literal
as world-view A, which is why Tillich calls this stage 'conscious literalism'. So the authority (in religious questions this
is often the Church or the Bible) supplies answers which for
a time (or sometimes for ever) suppress doubt, and provide
an alternative means whereby literal explanations can be
retained. The six days of Creation are explained perhaps as
six geological eras, so the notion of six days can be retained
alongside the geological evidence. A person's anxiety in the
face of such questioning is for the time being relieved.

Where questioning persists, or the answers provided do
not immediately or ultimately satisfy, Tillich suggests people
move to world-view C, which he calls 'broken myth and the
use of symbols'. Here, natural explanations (of Creation, for
example) can be accepted, but without losing sight of the
value of the myth, because the myth points beyond necessary
and important scientific and rational explanation to other,
ultimate concerns. 'Myth addresses the nature of the ultimate
while geology attends to that which is less than ultimate,
namely, the age of the earth.'[41] Such a view is not without its
anxiety, because myths and symbols do not provide certain

answers; but doubts are not resolved either by the magic explanations of literalism (world-view A) or by the sacred authority of conscious literalism (world-view B). Faith and courage (two of Tillich's key terms) conquer doubt, but they do not eliminate it. Such people learn to live with anxiety, with doubt and with ambivalence.

While Tillich's three world-views can be placed alongside Piaget's and Fowler's stages, personally I think that Tillich makes a huge jump when he moves from world-view B to world-view C. It is not difficult, for instance, to think of people who no longer accept symbols literally, and who are not content with the explanations of sacred authority, but who have no idea yet that myth and symbol might point to ultimate concerns. Myths are plainly 'not true', and there is no problem for them in that. They have not yet asked whether there might be another way of understanding myths. The person who holds world-view C is far removed from world-view B, and appears to have jumped at least one step along the way. For this reason, I place a question mark between world-views B and C, pushing the latter well into the second half of Fowler's chart (and indeed into the second half of life because I doubt if world-view C appears with much frequency before mid-life). Fowler's work, which helps to fill some of the gaps between world-view B and world-view C, seems to suggest that symbols and myths are not used in this creative but non-literal way until Stages 5 and 6.

The British theologian, Don Cupitt, also sets out a map that charts the development of religion, particularly forms of religious, philosophical or theological discourse, although he stays mainly within the Christian tradition.[42] I refer later in this book to some of his 'stages' of theological thinking, although at this point the parallels with other models might be seen in Cupitt's identification of 'mythical realism' (which is like world-view A) and 'doctrinal realism' which is like world-view B. The difference between his and Tillich's model is that Cupitt also describes formalized institutional attitudes.

Cupitt's analysis also supports a more individual psychology of belief. His approach is especially valuable because he is one of the few scholars who does not propose a single linear model: 'There is not one linear track running through three or four stations, as used to be thought in the past, but there are at any rate a large number of stations and a web of lines connecting them' which Cupitt sets out 'as a kind of Metro map of the spirit'.[43] His map is an important reminder of the dangers of seeing 'the journey of belief' as a single path, passing through definite stages in a predetermined order. I cannot divert here into the dilemmas posed by the idea of psychological determinism, or (in theological terms) pre-destination, although they represent important questions (as much in those disciplines as in philosophy). Whether, and to what extent, decisions and directions of a person's life journey are predetermined, the study of human development must always allow room for individual variations, arising from the infinitely large number of variables that influence any person's life.

Cupitt's Metro map is unusual in this respect. Although none of the models I have so far described *insists* on a rigidly linear scheme, there is nevertheless a temptation to link stages to ages, and to see each stage as being complete in itself. Fowler indicates that the ages spanned by most of his Stages of faith have blurred edges. Transitional periods apart, it is important to remember that all these models involve dynamic movement, and that they are not to be understood as static. They have all been developed from the perspective of *psychodynamic* psychology. If stages have some value as signposts of human growth, when it comes to real psycho-logical development, people pass into and out of (and back to as well as staying in) these various stages, depending upon external circumstances and upon their own internal responses to such eventualities.

Cupitt's model is still a journey, even if it is a circuitous and idiosyncratic one. The movement back and forth in attitudes and beliefs, which I prefer as a more accurate description of an individual's psychological path, is particularly well expressed in Hemenway's description of 'faith frame-works'.[44] She describes four types of theological and faith outlook. The first emphasizes the Fall, sin, evil, alienation and judgement. Rules feature strongly in this type of religion. The second is a theology which emphasizes redemption, and the triumph of good over evil. Christology, atonement, evangelism, and charismatic faith are all features of this framework. The third is typified by an emphasis on relation-ship and, in specific Judaeo-Christian terms, the covenant relationship throughout history between God and Israel, and

God and the Church. The Holy Spirit as seen as sustaining, and while there is still a sense of struggle between good and evil, there is also a belief in the developmental and historical unfolding of salvation. The last framework emphasizes unity in creation, and the acceptance of death as part of life—not as a defeat. There is more ecological and radical concern associated with this outlook than with the others.

These frameworks have resemblances to some of the stages in the models I have already considered. The first framework has similar features to religious belief and practice based upon rules and fear (Kohlberg's stage 1, Fowler's Stage 3 and Faber's anal religion). The second, with its interest in personal salvation, contains aspects which are reminiscent of the concern for self, seen in Kohlberg's moral stage 3 of self-interest; yet, in its tendency to enthusiasm and egocentricity, there are signs of the youthful energy that is typical of adolescence (Erikson's Age 5 and Faber's adolescent religion). The third shares in some respects the sense of community and concern for social order that features in Kohlberg's moral stage 4. Hemenway suggests that this particular framework indeed has much in common with the developmental approach which I have adopted here, and she mentions in that context, Fowler, Erikson and Piaget. The fourth framework resembles aspects of universalizing faith and universal principles in Fowler's and Kohlberg's Stage 6. In its more positive attitude towards death as the completion of life, there is much in common with Erikson's eighth Age, where integrity and wholeness also feature strongly.

Yet none of the four frameworks fit precisely into any of the developmental models. A feature here, an emphasis there, a parallel from one stage and yet a contradiction in another— all these would be apparent if I tried to line the four faith frameworks up with any of the columns in Fowler, Erikson, Piaget, Kohlberg or Tillich. This underlines Hemenway's observation that her model of faith frameworks is not developmental in nature. There is no sense in which someone moves 'back' to the first framework, or 'forward' to the fourth. Such thinking implies a value judgement that one framework is more 'healthy' than another.[45] Hemenway emphasizes that people move between these different frameworks, depending to some extent upon their mood. She links theological outlook to psychological feeling. She says that these frameworks have to be used multi-dimensionally, and she also suggests they can be seen as four strands that spiral together. Development and growth involve identifying them all, and gradually deciding which strands need to be developed, which discarded and which affirmed.

The shortcomings of models

Hemenway's approach, which urges the use of all the faith frameworks in understanding personal and faith development, is one which I want to endorse. If the wish for order draws us towards linear models, it is important to emphasize that at whatever stage a person is, especially in terms of their psychology of belief, none is any 'better' or 'worse' than another. The only qualification to this is that *within* each stage some forms of belief appear to be more positive for psychological health than others.

There is also a temptation to use any of the categories or stages outlined in this chapter to caricature, stereotype or label others, whether as individuals or *en masse*, belonging to groups of which for one reason or another we are suspicious or critical. Using knowledge to identify attitudes and beliefs can lead to better understanding, as the concept of 'naming' suggests, but naming arises out of intimate knowledge and in the context of care.[46] Hemenway admits that her own frameworks are over-simplified and somewhat stereotypical, and insists that they have to be used creatively, as jumping-off points to playing with ideas and perceptions.[47]

Some of the models I have reviewed are clearly linked to age and time: many people reach old age, where they inevitably face (if Erikson is right) issues of integrity versus despair. But others, such as Kohlberg's moral stages and Fowler's faith Stages, have to be understood as representing a journey which most people do not complete, however long they live. In most models, people reach a particular stage only by passing through the preceding ones: they do not, for instance, jump from level one in Kohlberg's scheme to level three, and then back to level two. But if the order is predictable, this does not rule out an important qualification in looking at any of these models, that at times people temporarily 'regress' (to use a psychoanalytic term) to earlier stages.

The shortcoming of these models is the possibility that, at different stages of development, not only are there features of earlier stages still present, but later stages are prefigured. There are particular links between first and last stages in both Erikson and Fowler, where the sense of being part of the universal in the last stage is prefigured in the awareness of and wish for continuing unity with the maternal figure in the first stage. I examine this more closely in Chapters 3 and 6.

A truly dynamic view of people allows for flexibility and fluidity. It draws upon models, but does not rigidly adhere to them. The models themselves describe parts, but not the whole. When we come to consider each individual (and I cannot rule out that the reader might want to consider himself or herself), we will inevitably find a mixed picture. The stage and state of a person's relationships, values, moral thinking and belief system, together and separately depend at any one time on many factors, such as the stimulation of events, of relationships, of education and of opportunity.

It is possible, therefore, for a sixty-year-old person to be at Kohlberg's stage 3 of moral thinking and Fowler's Stage 2 of faith development, whereas in physical and ego development (i.e. Erikson's model) he or she is working on the maturity issues of integrity versus despair. It is equally possible for a younger person in his mid-thirties to have had a number of short-lived sexual relationships (but stopping short of committing himself to the 'intimacy' that is typical of Erikson's sixth age of 'Young Adulthood'); and yet to gain immense satisfaction from his work as a teacher (thereby showing the creativity and generativity that is part of Erikson's seventh age). His moral thinking may be at Kohlberg's stage 5, and his faith development at Fowler's sceptical Stage 4. Or it is possible to think of a twenty-year-old student reading pure mathematics, who is physically mature and at the peak of physical fitness, whose intellectual capacity is such that she can work in the higher realms of conceptual thinking, and who in her moral thinking still functions at a pre-conventional level of fear and pleasing others. In her relationships, she may be very close to her friends, and in her faith development subscribe to a faith which is partly literal and completely conventional. She may therefore understand Creation as a beautiful and inspiring myth, but still believe literally in the virgin birth. No one fits into one narrow set of definitions.

These many levels of development are to some extent obscured by treating separately the parallel aspects for each of the themes, as I have chosen to do in Chapters 3 to 6. In most people various levels of development are at different stages, and yet they also bear upon one another. It is a complex task to identify where, at any one time, any one person may be in terms of their belief position. In any case, if Hemenway is right, what we think in the morning may be viewed differently by the time evening comes. The writer of Ecclesiastes was right: there is a time for everything.[48]

The analogy with which I started was that of a traveller walking across country to a mist-covered hill on the horizon. In this chapter, I have extended the possibilities of that journey, taking into account the temperament of the traveller, as well as the true nature of country which he or she has chosen to cross. To a large extent, the journey depends on the actual terrain through which he or she must pass. In planning the route, a walker often starts by drawing a straight line from start to finish, in order to map a rough path to the point of destination. But the line does not stay straight for long because the planned route needs to stay on footpaths and bridle-ways wherever possible; it must skirt lakes and impenetrable woods, and find the best place to cross rivers. The enthusiasm with which the walker turns the plan into action, or stays on course, depends to some extent upon temperament, which will in time also variously provide different satisfactions and frustrations along the way. Having started the walk, the traveller may find it necessary to backtrack occasionally when an unmapped obstacle appears, such as a ripe cornfield or a missing bridge. In the end the walker's route goes back and forth, while at the same time still making progress towards her or his destination.

The journey of belief is no different, but the chapters that follow may make it possible to identify some of the landmarks along the way.

Notes

1. J. W. Fowler, *Stages of Faith: the Psychology of Human Development and the Quest for Meaning* (San Francisco: Harper and Row, 1981), pp. 92–3. His definition of faith reads:

People's evolved and evolving ways of experiencing self, others and world (as they construct them) as related to and affected by the ultimate conditions of existence (as they construct them) and of shaping their lives' purposes and meanings, trusts and loyalties, in the light of the character of being, value and power determining the ultimate conditions of existence (as grasped in their operative images — conscious and unconscious — of them).

2. L. Kohlberg, *The Philosophy of Moral Development* (San Francisco: Harper and Row, 1981), p. 323.

3. W. Cantwell Smith, *Faith and Belief* (Princeton University Press, 1979), pp. 5-6.

4. R. C. Zaehner, *Hinduism* (Oxford University Press, 1962).

5. J. W. Fowler, *Stages of Faith*; *Becoming Adult, Becoming Christian* (San Francisco: Harper and Row, 1984); *Faith Development and Pastoral Care* (Philadelphia: Fortress Press, 1987).

6. Piaget's theories are set out thoroughly, with some of the questions raised by them, in J. L. Phillips, *The Origins of Intellect* (New York: W. H. Freeman, 1975).

7. C. Gilligan, *In a Different Voice: Psychological Theory and Women's Development* (Harvard University Press, 1982), pp. 10 and 18.

8. R. Goldman, *Religious Thinking from Childhood to Adolescence* (London: Routledge and Kegan Paul, 1964).

9. A. Harms, in Goldman, pp. 24-5.

10. Goldman, p. 25.

11. Kohlberg, *The Philosophy of Moral Development*.

12. Kohlberg, *The Philosophy of Moral Development*, p. 341. I draw upon this section of Kohlberg's book in the description of his moral stages.

13. L. Kohlberg, 'Education, Moral Development and Faith', *Journal of Moral Education*, 4:1, p. 14.

14. P. Tillich, *The Courage to Be* (New York: Nisbet, 1952).

15. Matthew 7. 10-11.

16. E. Erikson, *Childhood and Society* (London: Penguin Books, 1965), chapter 8.

17. S. Freud, *The Dissolution of the Oedipus Complex* (London: Penguin Freud Library), vol. 7, p. 320.

18. Gilligan, pp. 173-4.

19. M. Klein, 'On the theory of anxiety and guilt' in M. Klein, *Envy and Gratitude and Other Works 1946-1963* (London: Hogarth Press, 1975).

20. D. Capps, *Life Cycle Theory and Pastoral Care* (London: Fortress Press, 1983), p. 21.

21. M. Jacobs, *The Presenting Past* (Buckingham: Open University Press, 1986), pp. 7-8.

22. For the complete set *see* Jacobs, p. xiii.

23. E. Erikson, *Young Man Luther* (London: Faber & Faber, 1959); *Gandhi's Truth* (New York: Norton, 1969).

24. Capps examines how rituals can be used in the course of pastoral care, and there is a particularly interesting chapter on the pastor as 'The Ritual Co-ordinator'. *See also* H. P. V. Renner, 'The Use of

Ritual in Pastoral Care', *Journal of Pastoral Care*, 33:3 (1979), pp. 164–74. Renner draws upon Erikson's view of the basic roots of ritualization as coming from relationships between people.

25. F. Fordham, *An Introduction to Jung's Psychology* (London: Penguin Books, 1966), p. 78.

26. A. Samuels, *Jung and the Post-Jungians* (London: Routledge and Kegan Paul, 1985), chapter 5.

27. Fordham, p. 79.

28. Designed by I. Briggs Myers (Palo Alto, California: Consulting Psychologists Press, 1977).

29. H. Palmer, *The Enneagram: Understanding Yourself and Others in Your Life* (London: HarperCollins, 1991); O. Riso, *Practical Guide to Personality Types: Understanding the Enneagram* (London: Aquarian Press, 1988).

30. B. Bettelheim, *Freud and Man's Soul* (London: Chatto & Windus, 1983), p. 21.

31. S. Freud, *Three Essays on the Theory of Sexuality* (London: Penguin Freud Library), vol. 7, p. 122.

32. H. Faber, *Psychology of Religion* (London: SCM Press, 1976).

33. C. R. Badcock, *The Psychoanalysis of Culture* (Oxford: Blackwell, 1980).

34. See the chart summarizing his thesis in Badcock, p. 246.

35. Badcock, p. 249.

36. Badcock, p. 247.

37. Badcock, p. 249.

38. M. Jacobs, *The Presenting Past*. I now prefer the much shorter summaries of the themes in this text to those in *The Presenting Past*.

39. J. Robinson, *Honest to God* (London: SCM Press, 1963).

40. Fowler, *Stages of Faith*, pp. 92–3.

41. W. E. Baldridge and J. J. Gleason, 'A Theological Framework for Pastoral Care', *Journal of Pastoral Care*, 32:4 (1978), pp. 232–8. I draw my explanation of Tillich's world-views from this article, which can also be found in an abbreviated form in M. Jacobs, *Faith or Fear?* (London: Darton, Longman and Todd, 1987—now out of print). Tillich's world-views can be explored further in his book *Dynamics of Faith* (New York: Harper, 1957).

42. D. Cupitt, *Life Lines* (London: SCM Press, 1986).

43. Cupitt, p. 3. See his contents page for the map itself.

44. J. Hemenway, 'Four Faith Frameworks', *Journal of Pastoral Care*, 38:4 (1984), pp. 317–23. Also in Jacobs, *Faith or Fear?*, pp. 109–14.

45. Hemenway, p. 322.

46. See M. Jacobs, 'Naming and Labelling', *Contact*, 3 (1976); and Jacobs, *The Presenting Past*, pp. 22–4.

47. Hemenway, p. 317.

48. Ecclesiastes 3. 1–15.

PART TWO

Belief

THREE

Trust and Dependency

A complex collage

The desire to find order in what is otherwise a complex picture of human experience, and the wish to find parallels between various models of psychological development, at one time led me to create a chart which contained all the information I knew.[1] It was a personal indication of a frequent need in people generally, as the next chapter explains, to hold together apparent contradictions in a neatly ordered form; for a time my 'mega-model' suited my thinking. A few years on, it is interesting that I no longer wish to think that way. Instead, I prefer to take different elements from the models I outlined in the last chapter, and cluster them: in what Jung might have called 'a complex', and in what Freud might have called a series of 'associations'. Too much neatness masks the richness of these concepts.

In the chapters that follow, I describe a possible psychology of belief, based on four themes: the first three of which I take from the stages of childhood which Freud identifies. I take the three terms 'oral', 'anal' and 'genital' as being themselves metaphors: each one forms the matrix for a cluster of ideas, which helps make a collage of modes of belief. These modes may in some sense also be stages, although I have already expressed my caution about adopting too strict a linear model of 'development'. The technical terms and the symbols I collate point towards ways of understanding systems of belief.

Taking 'oral', 'anal' and 'genital' as three separate starting points, it is not surprising that Faber's study of the psychology of religion fits each picture immediately, because he also chose such a basis for his description of 'oral religion', 'anal religion' and 'genital religion'. His description of 'adolescent religion' I choose to attach to the 'genital' stage, but my explanation for that decision can wait for a later chapter. More immediately, Fowler's Stages of faith development can also be combined with Faber's scheme, and with the summary themes that I have myself proposed as most typical of the first three Freudian stages. The three 'core' modes of belief therefore become:

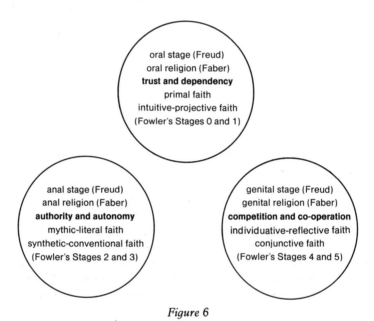

oral stage (Freud)
oral religion (Faber)
trust and dependency
primal faith
intuitive-projective faith
(Fowler's Stages 0 and 1)

anal stage (Freud)
anal religion (Faber)
authority and autonomy
mythic-literal faith
synthetic-conventional faith
(Fowler's Stages 2 and 3)

genital stage (Freud)
genital religion (Faber)
competition and co-operation
individuative-reflective faith
conjunctive faith
(Fowler's Stages 4 and 5)

Figure 6

The fourth and last theme of letting go, in Chapter 6, clusters aspects of the different models in a similar way, but does not take its cue from the early Freudian stages. It is related rather to Freud's concept of maturity, which includes seeing beyond illusions. Again, I will come to this all in good time. For the moment it is enough to start at the logical place, with the mother-baby relationship and with its importance for the foundation of the capacity for faith and belief.

Beginnings

Each of the three clusters above needs expanding to take full account of the richness of each of the models of development. Belief starts with the primary relationship of mother and baby, and this is reflected in the extension of 'Trust and Dependency' to include the other aspects identified in Figure 7.

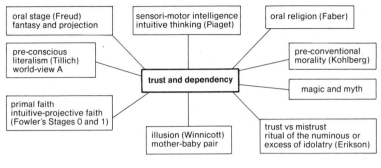

Figure 7

The language of psychoanalysis and the language of religion have much in common, which may be expected when both systems of thought and belief address 'something of the riddles of the world'.[2] In its own way, each lays considerable emphasis upon childhood — analysis, because it is in childhood that it is believed that the strengths and weaknesses that influence adult life are formed; and religion, because the attitude of true faith is often compared to that of becoming as a little child, or of being born again. The impetus given by psychoanalysis to the study of the way children 'understand' and experience life, together with child-centred education, has indeed demonstrated just how well children often see to the heart of things. Little wonder that Jesus is described as honouring children, and commending their kind of faith: 'Except you become as little children . . . who shall humble himself as this little child . . . who shall receive one such little child in my name'.[3] It is the more repressive apostle Paul who, while commending this imagery for some purposes (such as 'adoption as God's children',[4] and being 'followers of God as dear children'[5]) also hurries his readers into growing up by 'putting away childish things';[6] who constantly warns them about no longer being children, 'tossed to and fro and carried about with every wind of doctrine';[7] and who tells them not to be 'children in their understanding'.[8]

Mature psychological development involves negotiating the different stages of childhood and adolescence, and arriving at adult life without having lost touch with the child within. I shall come eventually to look at the value of the childlike capacity to 'play with ideas', by using the imagination at different levels of experience. In the first few years of life, there is a spontaneity of expression and a freedom in play, as well as an openness to the immediacy of present experience and feeling. This is one of the greatest gifts human beings ever have. Yet it can all too easily be forced underground or even eliminated by parental restrictions, or by the wrong kind of education, such as Dickens' schoolmaster Gradgrind, who saw children as 'little pitchers, who were to be filled so full of facts' that their 'tender young imaginations . . . were to be stormed away'.[9] Religion has also been used as a repressive agent to destroy children's enthusiasms.

In this chapter I undertake two tasks: one is to explain the way in which early experience forms the basis for adult faith and belief; the second is to describe forms of belief and practice which are related, even in adult life, to these early stages of life. I am not writing just about children (although their beliefs and ideas are fascinating and delightful); nor just about adults whose ideas and faith (at least in some respects) may to some people appear simple or even simplistic. These themes and experiences apply equally to those who have a more complex understanding of faith. It is difficult to avoid giving the impression, in combining these two objectives, that those who have a simple and a childlike faith are immature; or that features of belief which draw upon this early experience are in some way under-developed. Such value judgements are not my intention. One of the marks of Fowler's Stage 5 is the ability to accept where others are in the journey of belief. 'If where they are meets their needs sufficiently, we can affirm them and their world-view out of our own experience that . . . symbols once met all our needs and . . . remain meaningful to us'.[10]

For some people, what I describe here is a stage of belief on the way to a different level of perception; for others aspects of this type of belief remain in part alongside different ways of perceiving; while for many others (if we think in global terms) what I describe here is the only way people know of seeing the world and of experiencing their faith. I shall also follow Fowler's lead, in this and later chapters, in identifying ways in which some forms of belief in different stages become restrictive and anxiety-provoking, rather than provide richness and relief.

It is especially important to be clear that early stages of

development are never totally left behind, even though they are complemented and sometimes complicated by later factors. The main themes of the early stages of life continue to develop through childhood and adulthood. These themes (of trust, care, love, dependence and dependability) are linked to our first relationships, and are significant for everyone (even if sometimes in their absence). There are in fact similarities between this early stage of development and later stages of development. In this chapter, I examine the capacity people have shown for living (unconsciously) in the richness of their illusions. In later stages there are illusions of much the same kind, which are just as rich in their value: the difference is that people tend to have greater consciousness of the nature of their illusions in those stages. Using the Fowler model, there is a similarity therefore between people who are in these early Stages and those who are in Stages 5 and 6 (see also Chapters 5 and 6). People whose experience of belief and thinking fits into either these early or late Stages have in common an ability to make use of images and symbols in a way that is unrestricted, either by the necessity of having to be rational or by being excessively self-conscious.

There are clear differences between pre-conscious literalism (to use Tillich's world-view A), and belief systems which are more intellectually cognisant of—and yet also can use—'broken myth' and symbols (Tillich's world-view C). It may be that the illusions of the infant and the young child are hardly tested or informed by life experience, although many of those whose relatively 'simple faith' whom I describe are just as much in touch with the raw realities of life as those who apparently achieve greater insight. Although there are differences, there is more in common I believe between the uncomplicated beliefs and values of those who have 'simple faith' and the faith of those who have the benefit of more varied experience and wider knowledge, than there is between either group and those who express their beliefs in more ordered and tightly argued ways. Indeed, despite my efforts to be sympathetic to those whose belief and thought system is generally located in the middle Stages of the Fowler faith development model, I have a greater affection for these early Stages than for the more conventional ones that I describe in the next chapter. This is not based (as far as I am aware) upon any wish to regress to blissful ignorance (there is no reason to think infancy is that, let alone the lives of those whose beliefs happen to be less informed), as upon the sheer pleasure that comes from uncensored and unspoilt ways of experiencing and looking at the world.

The basis of trust

Trust, faith and belief are virtually synonymous. It makes sense that Erikson, in his attempt to develop a parallel for society of his model of individual development, should have equated the development of faith within society as a whole with the basic trust that is nurtured in a tiny baby. The earliest months and years of human life set the foundations for later life, and the experiences of a baby have a profound influence on the adult whom the child will eventually become. In particular, it is the experience of being nurtured, and the images formed initially of 'mother' (whoever does the nurturing) that continue to inform an adult's perception of self, of others and the world. Winnicott describes it in this way:

> It is especially at the start that mothers are vitally important, and indeed it is a mother's job to protect her infant from complications that cannot yet be understood by the infant, and to go on steadily providing the simplified bit of the world which the infant, through her, comes to know.[11]

The sense of trust which is built (or not built) in primary relationships, influences later values, attitudes and faith. The quality of these early relationships promotes (or does not promote) both the affirmation of the first stirrings of the self and, at the same time, an early ability to empathize and identify with other people. In turn, this forms the basis for moral development that moves beyond self-interest and externalized imperatives towards genuine concern.

Many images which people have of God (or the gods) are projections from early experience, although this is no more a comment on their validity than is describing the use of many phrases in the English language as metaphorical. Language often has to use other means than the literal of expressing thoughts and feelings in graphic terms. Abstract ideas and concepts may be intellectually correct, but they are less than complete in their ability to evoke the full measure of experience. There is however a difference between the use of metaphor in the different stages or modes of belief, which might be described as between:

1. Those who do not realize they are using language in this way (and for whom it is in any case not relevant)
2. Those who are wary of admitting that they are using metaphor lest they appear to undermine the credibility of their faith (those who wish to be seen as correct and who therefore tend to support literalism uncritically)
3. Those who, if they reflect on their use of metaphor or are invited to explain what they mean, know they are not speaking literally, but who still enjoy the richness that comes from the use of language at different levels at once.

Images from the earliest relationship of mother and child colour the growing and developing world of a child. This happens because this initial experience is the *only* world a baby knows. At first, there is nothing dividing baby and mother. What appears to the observer as such a tiny world is actually the whole world for a baby; and, in the first instance, there is no other world to correct or extend the crucial picture that is built up in the first few weeks of life. As an infant's world expands, the world that enlarges with it is the one that the baby originally perceived. It therefore colours all later experiences, which are then incorporated by being accommodated into what the baby already knows. Just as a picture on a rubber balloon expands in size as the balloon is blown up, so the bigger a child's world grows, the larger (if fainter) grow the original perceptions that are attached to it. The initial picture or perception, as it grows larger, interprets the wider world as more of the same: where early experience has been good, the expanding world tends to be seen as good; equally the world may appear even more terrifying, if early nurturing has left the scars of negative images. Later experiences sometimes correct early impressions, although these experiences may just as easily confirm early impressions, making some of them seem almost indelible (for good or for ill). For most people, in the course of growing up, the world becomes a place where they pass through good and bad experiences: some of them are welcome, some of them could be better done without: but we learn to accept an ambivalent attitude to the world around us.

The expanding boundaries of a child's world begin to take in other people, other experiences and other ideas, including the spiritual and the cognitive. These are all open to being interpreted or coloured by early experience. Pictures of God are no exception, and for many people their God remains a projection of some aspect of their early childhood experience. His appearance (God's gender tends to be male, especially when there is only one god as there is in monotheistic religions) or his qualities are by and large taken from human beings, and often from parental images. The exception is in animistic forms of religion, where other elements of the natural world are employed as images of the gods.

Freud was not the first person to point out that the figure of God meets the needs of a child. He states the following:

> The terrifying impression of helplessness in childhood aroused the need for protection—for protection through love—which was provided by the father; and the recognition that this helplessness lasts throughout life made it necessary to cling to the existence of a father, but this time a more powerful one.[12]

Earlier than Freud, the nineteenth-century philosopher Feuerbach had suggested that God is nothing more than a projection of human imagination. Before Freud's first paper on the subject appeared, Jack London in his novel *White Fang* had penned a similar view of projection, which almost anticipates Freud's psychological explanation of the phenomenon: '. . . man, whose gods are of the unseen and of the overguessed, vapours and mists of fancy eluding the garmenture of reality, wandering wraiths of desired goodness and power, intangible outcroppings of self into the realm of spirit'.[13] Freud's thesis lays more stress on the 'child' than the 'man': that the child in the adult needs to perpetuate an image of an omniscient and omnipotent parent, which the child is forced to give up when she recognizes that parents are fallible and imperfect. God can therefore be seen as a type of super-parent, who imparts a sense of order and protection and security in a hostile world. God goes on looking after us, long after our parents have ceased literally to do so.

What is fascinating is that even if God is normally 'male'

and 'Father', the images used of him are frequently maternal. In much of his writing, Freud emphasizes the role of the father over and above that of the mother. It may therefore be a reflection of the heavily patriarchal society in which he lived, and of the religion of his childhood, that he should identify God as a father-figure, although we cannot rule out that he may have had more problems with his mother than he was publicly prepared to admit, and that this prevented him from looking more deeply both at the significance of motherhood and of maternal images of God. Nevertheless, he thought that the great mother-goddesses perhaps preceded the father-gods.[14]

It was Freud's followers who suggested that greater emphasis should be given to the study of the mother-baby relationship, and to the essential foundation which this provided for later development: it is their studies that have in turn extended our understanding of expressions of faith and belief. As I have already explained, although Freud described the first stage of psycho-sexual development as 'the oral stage', it was Erikson who extended the idea of trust — as the essential issue in that stage of development — to faith as well. Fowler also lays stress on the mother-child relationship when he identifies Stage 0 as 'primal faith'. In refusing to give the stage a definite number he perhaps wishes to represent faith in its very earliest stage as incapable of a proper identity, partly because (as I have described already) an infant cannot yet be easily separated from the mother-baby relationship; and partly because faith is, in the term he uses to encapsulate Stage 0, 'undifferentiated'. Similarly, Fowler hypothesizes that the early months give rise to what he calls the first *pre-images* of God: 'pre-' because as yet there is no language to describe them. These pre-images emerge from the experience of the mutual relationship of mother and baby, in which a baby has the first awareness of a rudimentary sense of self, which is separate from and yet dependent upon others.[15] Agreeing with Winnicott, Erikson and psychoanalytic opinion generally, Fowler sees this initial period as one where the seeds of trust, courage, love and hope are sown. Faber, who draws heavily upon Erikson, similarly suggests that the relationship with the mother is essential for the capacity to trust, to believe, and (he quotes Tillich's phrase) 'the courage to be'. He also stresses the need for trust to be built up if the child is to become emancipated from the mother, and to move from dependence to independence. Drawing on the German term *Befriedigung* that Freud uses to describe the mother-child relationship at its best, Faber observes that the word not only means 'satisfaction' but also contains an echo of 'peace' — and that psychologists also describe the satisfied child as in a state of 'bliss', originally, as Faber says, a religious term.[16]

Maternal images in experience and belief

A study of hospital patients' views of God (I presume that they were mental hospital patients, although this is not clear in the report) showed a significant correlation in their group (and a non-significant correlation for a control church group) that God is identified in terms of their actual parents. It also showed that mothers figure just as greatly as fathers in people's perceptions of God.[17] Similarly, a preliminary study which I conducted many years ago (using male theological college students) also hinted that their construct of God was closely related to their construct of an ideal mother.

There is a danger, particularly since I write as a man, of sentimentalizing and idealizing motherhood. Much explicit religious imagery already does this, although as I shall also show there are images which demonstrate the other side of the picture, especially where a baby fears the devouring punitive mother — a projection sometimes of the baby's own wish to 'eat her up'. Winnicott knew mothers and babies well enough to realize that another side of the experience of nurturing and being nurtured cannot be forgotten, when he writes of the mother's hate for her baby; for example, 'the baby is an interference with her private life, a challenge to preoccupation . . . He is ruthless, treats her as scum, an unpaid servant, a slave'.[18] Mature thinking and comprehensive belief should certainly embrace the less idealized experiences of infancy.

We do not have to look far for symbols and images, used in describing religious and mystical experience, that confirm the view of the writers on psychological development that early infancy is significant for the development of faith. There are strong elements in all religions (although in some more explicitly than in others, and particularly in the Catholic expression of Christianity) that are drawn from these maternal and nurturing images and symbols. God is described as provider and sustainer of life: feeding and comforting are characteristic features of the divine. In primitive or naturalistic religion, the nurturing and sustaining function is often expressed in terms of earth goddesses; in animistic religion there is a sense of intimate unity with the natural world, the womb of humankind.

In different religious traditions, communion with the divine and with other worshippers takes place through the act of feeding. This symbolism is particularly profound within the Christian tradition and ritual of the Eucharist. The traditional symbol for Corpus Christi is the female pelican suckling her young from the blood drawn from her own breast; the parallel to a human mother's breast is plain enough; and probably one of the most psychologically powerful phrases in the whole of Christian liturgy is that used in consecration and distribution of the bread: 'This is my Body'. The parallel is with a mother offering her breast to her baby, in an act that in some way might well be experienced by a baby as equally sacrificial and sacred. The context and content of public worship also 'feeds' people in all sorts of ways, helping to meet their wishes for dependency and dependability, wishes for closeness with the transcendent and with others, wishes to be accepted and wishes to be loved. The heights of religious experience are sometimes expressed as a state of bliss, that is reminiscent of the symbiotic unity of mutual love that can exist between a mother and her baby. The analyst Balint used the delightful phrase 'primitive, harmonious, inter-penetrating mix-up' of the relationship of the nursing couple, and this might just as well also describe the mystical relationship.[19]

The wish for unity and harmony is seen in other ways than through religious experience alone. The relationship with nature (particularly in the Romantic poets such as Wordsworth) evokes similar images. Music (which includes sacred music, but is by no means confined to it) is a particularly evocative form of expression, perhaps because its medium of communication is non-verbal: like the earliest form of vocal communication between mother and baby, music 'speaks' through sound, tone and rhythm, and not in words. Harmony (in music, of the spheres, and so on) represents the joy and beauty which is also found in symbiotic unity. Another form of this unity and harmony is found in mathematics where, for example, powerful computers search for the highest prime number (whole numbers that cannot be divided by other whole numbers, such as 1, 2, 3, 5, 7, 11 and so on). Such numbers have their own fascination and excitement, but the idea of indivisibility may be psychologically powerful as well. At another level, mathematical thinking is also about order and sets (and therefore akin to the themes included in the next chapter). It also involves abstract thinking that is both complex and yet possesses (to those that understand it) a purity and simplicity that gives playing with numbers and formulae a rare kind of beauty. While some of this thinking has parallels with the complex thinking that I examine in the final chapter, it also carries hints of a search for wholeness (rather than the neatness that might be typical of the next stage) which is reminiscent of the belief system contextualized in this chapter.

It might also be relevant to stand this imagery of unity and bliss with the mother on its head. Not only does much mystical language appear to represent a wish to return to the unity of the mother-baby relationship, but mothering itself may at times be a similarly spiritual and harmonious experience. Danah Zohar writes of her pregnancy:

> I experienced what for me was a strange new way of being. In many ways, I lost the sense of myself as an individual, while at the same time gaining a sense of myself as part of some larger and ongoing process.

> At first the boundaries of my body extended inwards to embrace and become one with the new life growing inside me. I felt complete and self-contained, a microcosm within which *all* life was enfolded.

> I experienced myself as extending in all directions, backwards into 'before time' and forwards into 'all time', inwards towards all possibility and outwards towards all existence.[20]

Not all pregnancies are like this, but this and other aspects of mothering are clearly spiritual experiences in themselves.

Even if God is frequently portrayed in the Judaeo-Christian tradition as a distant and stern father-figure (and occasionally more positively as the forgiving father running out to meet the prodigal) other religions place greater emphasis upon the feminine in the Godhead or in the pantheon of the gods. Even within the Judaeo-Christian tradition, feminist theologians have made us look again at the latent images that show the feminine side of God that counterbalance the masculine images, which have dominated the Christian (and also the Muslim) tradition.[21] Seeing the Godhead as inclusive of both genders is not simply a modern phenomenon. Dame Julian of Norwich saw the motherhood of God at work in Creation, and called Jesus 'Mother of mercy'.[22] Meister Eckhart uses a feminine form for the Godhead. More commonly within the Christian tradition, the figure of Mary has been the closest approximation to a mother God—hence the discomfort of most Protestants about the particular devotion which Catholics express towards her. Perhaps a psychological objection would be rather to the idealization of the state of motherhood, which achieves full flower in the generally sanitized pictures of a gentle Mary. The reality of mothering, with its pain and frustrations as well as its joys, is almost totally ignored. The *Pietà*—the image of the mother of Jesus at the foot of the cross holding the body of her dead son—is the nearest we get to an expression of the depth of pain that is equally part of motherhood.

It is this sometimes exaggerated and idealized imagery of the Virgin-mother and Child that might tempt us to follow Freud and make the reductive interpretation that maternal symbolism in religious thought and experience is simply an example of wish-fulfilment. In Freud's more negative view of these matters, the oceanic feeling that is experienced in religious ecstasy is the wish to regress to the deepest moments of unity in the mother-baby symbiosis—to Balint's 'primitive harmonious interpenetrating mix-up'. But Winnicott's version of illusion is more helpful here, and is echoed independently by Erikson who sees such experience more positively. He writes of 'the simple and fervent wish for a hallucinatory sense of unity with the maternal matrix'.[23] In the same context, he sees no reason for it to be called regression if 'man thus seeks again the earliest encounters of his trustful past in his efforts to reach for a hoped-for and eternal future'. At its best, the wish for unitary experience and the belief in its possibility, in Erikson's opinion, helps us to return to early experience, to work at setting right some of the issues that

concerned us then and still concern us now. I explore another
identical view in relation to mystical experience in Chapter 6.

In the last chapter, I mentioned how Erikson has identified
'rituals' that are connected with each of his 'eight Ages'. By
'ritual' he does not simply mean sacred rites and ceremonies,
but also the social rituals which form part of the life of a
community. In connection with the oral stage, Erikson
identifies the numinous (sense of the holy) aspect of ritual. In
sacred rites, the numinous is often invoked in the act of
looking or being looked upon. In some ceremonies, only the
priest is allowed to enter the Holy of Holies — although this
may actually heighten the sense of the numinous in those
who are not permitted to 'see' within. In other ceremonies,
the act of looking is encouraged — for example, in the elevation
of the host, or in the use of sacred icons and images — all of
which helps promote the sense of the numinous, both in
looking and being looked upon.

This sense of the numinous is closely linked by Erikson to
the relationship between mother and baby, which also
involves gazing, responding to, and being looked at and
smiled upon. The act of looking is a vital means of
communicating, because in this pre-verbal stage words are
meaningless except as expressing tones of voice, which
themselves convey feelings. It is in seeing and being seen that
a baby is helped to overcome her fear of separation and
isolation. In religion too, although the numinous in one sense
suggests a distance between the worshipper and the god, it is
the numinous aspect of ritual which also helps overcome a
person's sense of isolation from his or her god.

Such ritualization is positive in Erikson's opinion, although
he also describes a more negative form, which he calls 'ritual
excess'. This tends to lead to poor social relationships and to
false religion. There is an equivalent ritual excess for each of
the eight forms of ritualization. In his idea of ritual excess,
Erikson is in some agreement with Freud, who was himself
very critical of religious ritual, comparing it to obsessional
actions.[24] In relation to the oral stage and the ritual of looking,
the ritual excess is idolatry, the reverse side of the numinous.
Although Erikson refers to idolatry in religious terms, with
objects being treated like gods, an equivalent idolatry is
present in human relationships, where it is also known in

psychological terms as idolizing or idealizing. Objects or people take the place of the numinous; and in psychological terms, one of the effects of idealization is a weakening rather than a strengthening of the sense of self. Idealization, as I explain below, is prone to emphasize the gap between oneself and the divine. Idealization of another (whether a person or sacred object or a god) is invariably at the idealizer's expense.

In Winnicott's identification of the 'transitional object', there is a similar possibility which fits with this 'ritual excess', which Erikson describes as idolatry. From the first chapter, the reader may recall that Winnicott states how important it is for a mother to help her baby find a transitional object — one which gives the baby the necessary illusion of power and control. While the breast may be the first transitional object, generally Winnicott means this term to be a dummy, a cuddly toy, a piece of muslin or blanket (or a similar object), which is 'not-me' and which is not attached to the baby (the thumb is not strictly a transitional object), and so can be put down and found again. In the end, although this may take much longer for some children than others, the transitional object is given up — or largely given up — inasmuch as it no longer has the same illusory power that it once had. It may still have many fond associations with childhood, and therefore be retained as a keepsake, like an old and battered favourite teddy. But if a child does not eventually give up the transitional object, Winnicott says that it becomes like a fetish, and it fosters delusion. Since, in Winnicott's opinion, some kind of transitional object (such as through art and religion) is always necessary, even into adult life, he must be referring to 'the persistence of a specific object or type of object dating from infantile experience in the transitional field' when he makes the distinction between transitional objects in a positive sense, and a fetish (or idol?) in the more negative sense.[25]

Like Erikson, I would not want to label as neurotic or regressive the type of religious or spiritual imagery and experience that expresses some kind of wish to return to the blissful times of infancy. Whether it is in the religious sphere, or in the wider experience of cultural expression — especially in the arts — these images and symbols are important to us (and to our psychological health), even if there is always a danger, as Erikson's 'ritual excesses' remind us, that images can become idols and symbols can become substitutes. The Garden of Eden, the myth tells us, was strongly guarded by cherubim with the flaming sword: it is actually impossible to return for long to such states of pure happiness.[26]

Idealization

The ideal state of bliss or 'reverie' (as Winnicott describes one aspect of the mother-baby relationship) cannot be sustained for long. We also have to be careful about idealizing objects—people, gods, beliefs, or systems of thought—whether it be in a religious sphere of activity, or in other frames of reference. Religious figures become screens upon which wishes, fears and prejudices are projected. The danger is that, in so doing, values and principles are reified (made into something real and objective), when they are in fact still fluid and open to doubt.

The newly 'converted' are particularly prone to this. (It is the danger of Fowler's Stage 4, as we shall see.) They idealize their new found conviction, whether it is in Jesus, the Pope, Freud, Carl Rogers, in a political party, or a system of thought (such as Zen, humanism, behavioural psychology, 'science', and so on). The ease with which people set up gods is demonstrated in the cargo cults in the Pacific, 'whose members built tin-can replicas of aircraft, believing that they could thus magically reproduce the wonders of supply of good things from the skies'.[27] The reification of belief is likely to stifle it in the end. Which Jesus, for example, should Christians believe in? The compassionate friend? The zealous and angry radical? The liberal? The teacher? The person who refused to be called 'Master'? The listener or the prophet? The messianic figure? The god or the man? The quest for Jesus, whether it is the historical, the psychological or the theological Jesus will end up as the individual historian's, the individual psychologist's and the individual theologian's Jesus.

Similar cautions about identifying and idealizing are true of other faiths. Shah makes the point about the Sufis that despite personality-worship being forbidden, 'such is the attraction of personality to the ordinary man, that the successors of Sufi teachers have tended to produce, rather than a living application of the principles taught, hagiographies and bizarre and deficient systems'.[28] Watts writes of followers of the Buddha that 'they have revered and depended upon the records of his sayings as if they enshrined his wisdom, yet in so doing they have made those records not only a shrine but the tomb in which the dead carcass of his wisdom is buried'.[29] Harding observes that though, like Jesus, Buddha was a historical person, this does not prevent a Zen master from writing that 'the real Buddha has no mouth and preaches no Dharma' (a deliberately ambiguous term which means, variously, 'properties', 'teachings', 'true facts', 'real events', and so on).[30] Fromm says much the same about the followers of Freud, that they 'were mostly pedestrian men . . . They needed a dogma in which they could believe and around which they could organize the movement . . . Freud the teacher became the prisoner of his faithful, but uncreative disciples'.[31]

Avoiding reality

Over-idealization may lead to the ignorance or avoidance of another kind of 'reality'. There is another side to the experience of infancy and of mothering that is far removed from any idealized picture, and yet it is also an aspect of systems of belief. The frustrating and painful side of infancy is a corrective to dwelling too much on images of harmony and bliss.

Fowler reminds us of this other side to the experience of infancy, when he expands his picture of undifferentiated faith to include the point at which all babies each have to contend with the threat of abandonment, inconsistency and deprivation (whether in fact or in their fantasy). He uses a theological term to describe this experience, calling it a fall from grace, a type of primal Fall into consciousness, as babies realize that they are not at the centre of the world, that they need others, and that others are separate beings who are not at their omnipotent command. Psychoanalytic thought certainly concurs that the dawning of this realization occurs when a baby begins to perceive that mother is a separate person, and not always 'on tap'. Primal bliss inevitably has to alternate with experiences of deprivation, which might at times be as close to hell as 'a good feed' is to heaven: the contrast is vividly portrayed in the story of Dives' thirsting in hell, and looking up to Lazarus 'in Abraham's bosom'.[32] The breast, which the baby so much needs and desires for psychological as well as physical reasons, sometimes provides succour and a sense of well-being. At other times, however, the same breast is withheld, giving rise to a totally different set of experiences in the child, which are reflected in extreme cases in adult experiences of complete emptiness and lack of self-worth.

The sublimity of Fowler's Stage 0 ('primal and undifferentiated faith') inevitably has to give way to different experiences, which start a child on the road towards facing both the reality of the separateness of the world and of others, and the frustration that is just as much part of life as satisfaction. Trust, according to Faber, includes more than ultimate security and the capacity to receive love; it also involves delight in reality, the integration of negative experiences, and the capacity not to be overwhelmed by fear or aggression.[33] We have seen also how Winnicott describes the mother's task not only as one of creating a sense of illusion for her baby, the illusion that the baby has control of the breast, but also as disillusioning her baby later on, so that her baby can begin to learn to tolerate reality. It is this other side of the picture which deserves our attention because, at whatever stage of belief a person may function, integrity involves being able to hold together the light and the shadow (to use Jung's terms), or good and bad experiences (in more psychoanalytic language). In religious terms, it may also be described as the problem of integrating personal good and evil. While it has to be conceded that this is a lifelong task, it is begun in infancy and can be helped or hindered by particular types of faith and belief.

The inability to face frustrations, the fear of *angst* and aggression, of sexuality and tenderness and the impossibility of reconciling good and bad experiences can lead to distortions in psychological functioning, as well as to less than healthy beliefs. In his discussion of oral religion, Faber reminds us that a failure of trust can lead to different experiences of the mother (as bad) and to a different set of fantasies, which still have an oral (feeding) character. One such fantasy, as I have briefly indicated above, is the fear of being devoured. This fear is reflected in fairy tales where children are abandoned by their parents (often by mother), and are at risk of being devoured by some evil figure like a witch, giant or wolf. The same anxious imagery is present in phrases used in religious imagery such as 'the jaws of death' or the 'jaws of the grave'. Another phrase, familiar from the New Testament and to some as part of the monastic night office (said just before going to bed, when sleep might be compared to a sort of death) speaks of being 'wary of the devil who, like a lion, prowls around seeking whom he may devour'. Faber also observes that death does not have to be seen in such terrifying ways, but can be expressed in the more comforting terms from oral imagery, such as the tomb being equated with the womb.[34]

Failure to trust (based on experiences in childhood) may also lead to terrifying pictures of God. Justice and Lambert illustrate how incest victims can have a distorted view of God and of God's love—demonstrating, incidentally, how dangerous it might be to try to use apparently comforting images of God when counselling people who have been abused. They quote one woman as saying to her minister: 'When I hear you say that God loves me, I have a hard time trying not to remember Daddy raping me and saying, "I love you, I love you, I love you all"—all the time he was doing it to me . . . Even after all these years, every time I hear the word God, I see Daddy's face'.[35]

This bleak picture is a less comforting example of the influence of childhood experiences on the formation of images of God. With such negative experiences of trust, we can see how some forms of unbelief, mistrust, cynicism and 'bad faith' might result from experience of the bad times in infancy. Faber refers to a study of the psychology of unbelief, in which the author (Rumke) argues that it is unbelief, and not belief, which indicates a disturbance in development.[36] Given the broad definition of faith and belief which is used throughout this book, there seems every possibility that the psychological difficulty of believing 'in anything' is the result of lack of a trusting environment in infancy and childhood.

Fowler makes good use of the image of the 'fall from grace' when he described what happens to babies within the first few months of life. Unlike the Garden of Eden myth, what he describes is no one's *fault*, but an inevitable part of growing consciousness. He suggests two negative directions in which faith might develop from the 'primal faith' Stage 0. One consists of the feelings of isolation and mistrust I have alluded to above. The other is excessive narcissism, where the baby's need to be at the centre of everything continues to dominate, and where the fantasy persists in some forms of belief (for example, that God or the gods are at one's beck and call). In its most extreme form, it is seen in those who claim divinity for themselves—often people who are described as having psychotic or borderline personalities, where they appear not to be able to separate from the omnipotent object to which they still wish to be attached. There is also a narcissistic element in the way some people try to make others clones of themselves: they wish to pressurize and convert others to the same beliefs as themselves. This type of enthusiasm is an undiluted acting out of the delusion of 'the god within', which is what the word 'enthusiasm' originally meant. Similarly, fanaticism tends to boost egotism more than its cause. For people who show these traits, resistance to their demands, or the failure of their god to answer their prayers, can lead to an even greater wound to their pride. Their self-esteem is based on the narcissistic wish for others to please them, and is not founded on a genuine sense of self-worth. The zeal to convert, which I describe here, is different in quality from that rather more pedestrian (though still repressive) feature of what Faber calls 'anal religion', which wants to make everyone conform—but since the pressure to conform is to help preserve the institution, perhaps there is a kind of parallel between the need to preserve the self-esteem of the institution on the one level, and that of the narcissistic believer on another: both institution and individual may find separateness or difference threatening.

There are other ways of reacting to the situation which Fowler portrays, in which dawning consciousness is felt in some way like a 'fall from grace'—expulsion from the bliss or reverie of the Garden of Eden. In psychodynamic psychology, one such reaction is technically known as splitting. This term describes the attempt to cope with the enormous difficulty a baby has of comprehending (what adults come to know) that good and bad experiences can arise from the same source (i.e. from the same mother or the same 'breast', as Winnicott and others express it). One way of understanding such a contradiction is to imagine that there must be one bad mother (or bad breast) responsible for all the frustration and pain; and another mother (or good breast) who is responsible for all the satisfaction and love. In healthy development during infancy, extreme splitting gradually gives way to ambivalence and to the realization that good and bad experiences come from the same source. Some analysts believe that this realization gives rise to constructive and reparative guilt, to concern and to hope, as long as the good is felt to outweigh the bad. On the other hand, despair or paranoid feelings might result when the bad seems stronger than the good.

Here, in psychological form, is one of the most taxing of all theological questions. How can a good God (like a good mother) allow bad things to happen? Splitting is seen in faith terms wherever there is dualistic belief — the belief in two gods, one of whom is good and the other of whom is evil. Despite its apparent monotheism, Christianity has sufficient evidence of such dualism in its art and literature, portraying the struggle between God and the Devil. This dualism is also seen in ancient near eastern Creation myths. It is also evident wherever people see their own souls as the battleground for the powers of good and evil.

There are serious philosophical and theological questions about the relationship between good and evil, which I do not wish to belittle. But, in psychological terms, some of the solutions that people arrive at are less than satisfactory. More mature thinking (psychologically) requires the acceptance of ambivalence. Such a way of perceiving others, gods, God, fate or even life itself may be just as apparent (indeed sometimes more apparent) in those whose faith we may be tempted otherwise to describe as 'simple'. There is no reason why healthy ambivalence should not be part of what Tillich calls 'pre-conscious literalism'. Baldridge and Gleason give an example of a person who holds what they describe as Tillich's world-view A.[37] She is a grandmother who has lost nearly all her family in a tragic succession of deaths. Yet she can still say with complete conviction that what has happened is all God's will, and that 'the Lord is good' to her. What makes her simple faith so mature is that she does *not* see the deaths of her relatives as any kind of punishment, or as the work of the Devil. There is no sense in which she says 'God is good and I am bad, and I deserve what has happened to me'; nor 'God is good, it is the devil who is bad and has done all this'. Instead she holds together her tragic experience with a good God, providing a superb example of the way in which a literal, undeveloped and unquestioning faith can sometimes express just as mature a psychological attitude as a more complex and well-argued solution to the problem of evil. The elderly woman's simple faith gives her the ability to reconcile bad experiences with a good God, and at the same time helps her retain a sense of her own self-worth.

It may be that she (and others like her) are able to hold contradictions together, such as the life and death issues she experienced, because her thinking and her belief in Piaget's terms is still largely intuitive. She is unable to be concerned about more than one aspect of her situation: in a sense the contradictions do not occur to her. There may be a difference between ambivalence where it is largely not thought out, and ambivalence that results from strenuous wrestling with the problems of contradiction and paradox, which is more typical of Fowler's Stage 5 and of higher levels of abstract thought. I am not familiar enough with Hindu thought to be sure of a parallel there, but I detect a primitive type of ambivalence in relation to some of the early gods, such as Indra, who both destroys yet also recreates order; or Veruna, who is the guardian of truth yet also resorts to guile. I notice a more complex ambivalence in relation to the more developed figure, the god Shiva, who is 'the reconciliation of all opposites: therefore he is both creator and destroyer, terrible and mild, evil and good, male and female, eternal rest and ceaseless activity'.[38]

This psychological task of unifying experience, and of integrating good and bad, which also has impact on different forms of belief, is not one that psychologists expect to be resolved in infancy, although it is in infancy and childhood that the process is begun. These issues continue to present themselves at all points of life. Adolescents often alternate rapidly between elation and despair, taking a long time to recognize that the presence of one does not mean the total absence of the other. Those who fall in love have to work through their mutual idealization to be able to integrate the less attractive realities which they also see in each other. Parents soon learn that they both do adore and yet could murder their babies; that their children can be angels and also devils. In the ageing process, people often reflect upon their lives, upon the good and bad moments, the successes and failures, the joys and the disappointments. The ability to accept and contain ambivalent feelings about life experiences makes it less likely that either the positive or the negative will get split off and ignored.

Moving towards symbols

Winnicott draws a useful distinction between transitional objects and symbols. A transitional object is treated *as if* it were the object itself. In using symbols, we are able to distinguish fact from fantasy. The point of a transitional object is not its symbolic value, but 'its actuality', whereas symbols stand only for something else.[39] Such differences are helpful in identifying the forms of belief in symbols which different people may have — some using symbols as transitional objects, and others aware that their images and symbols need not be taken literally. Symbols are a means of seeing through to something else. They are a shorthand, a quick way through to the less explicable or to the less readily identifiable. Having to explain them, renders them tautologous and somewhat useless. Nevertheless, if they are asked, those who recognize that they are using symbols are at least able to identify them as such.

The discovery of the value of symbols is an important step forward. It opens up greater possibilities for playing with ideas and problems. Symbols are extremely valuable and make concepts more manageable, for example, to a mathematician or scientist in shortening the amount of work to be done. In the developing psychology of belief, symbols are the next step; away from the maternal relationship, towards a more direct way of handling the world of experience.

Fowler's next Stage in his faith development model, is the first definitely numbered: Stage 1, a stage of 'intuitive-projective faith'. The continuous process of perception that starts here merges to some extent with Stage 2, since both stages draw amply upon symbols and images. The difference in Fowler's eyes is that Stage 2 consists more of *ordering* symbols into more complete myths and stories. Nevertheless, hard and fast distinctions are not easy, and there is an overlap between some of what I touch on in this chapter, as well as some of what I include at the start of the next. While Stage 1 is not chronologically co-terminous with Erikson's first Age, there are many features in Fowler's description of it which show psychological similarities with Erikson's oral stage: as in Stage 0, there are also themes of trust and dependency here. Stage 1 is typified by the first discovery of a sense of self. Fowler includes in this Stage the way children ask a host of questions; although whether the answers they receive are the ones they want is not always obvious to an adult. Children in this Stage have difficulty both in understanding the relation between cause and effect, and in maintaining more than one perspective on experience at a time (again we see here examples of Piaget's stage of intuitive thinking). This may help us to understand how an adult's incomplete answers still satisfy the child's enquiring mind.

From what little we can know of infants' thoughts before they can describe them, children struggle to make sense of their experience, even before they can frame their questions in words. With the advent of language, explanations can be more easily sought and more easily given. Some children's questions appear very deep, although the obvious ease with which they can often be satisfied by a simple, intelligible answer makes the purpose of the original question far from clear. I have shown above, in the example of the grandmother who did not question the tragic deaths in her family as a sign of the absence of a good God, that there are some people whose deep questions appear to be equally readily answered. Their world-view A is able to contain their anxiousness, and they do not need to seek for explanation or proof or quasi-historical truth in a way that is more typical of the person who holds Tillich's world-view B.

Fowler describes Stage 1 as a time that is filled with fantasy, where a child is powerfully and permanently influenced by examples, moods, actions and stories coming from adults. With unrestrained imagination, and uninhibited by logical thought as adults understand it, a child at this Stage grasps the world of experience intuitively. Fairy stories, and certain religious stories, may help the movement towards the ambivalence that I have described above, supporting the child's belief that good wins over bad. Many stories end with what Tolkien calls a 'eucatastrophe' in which everything is turned over for *good*.[40] The danger of this Stage is that a child's imagination becomes possessed by unrestrained and uncorrected images of terror and destructiveness. Adults or older siblings may exploit a child's imagination, reinforcing taboos and moral and doctrinal obligations with images of punishment, the devil and death. Religion, through its potent symbols, is one of the most obvious ways in which this repressive force is exercised, as, for example, in the fire and brimstone sermon in Joyce's *A Portrait of the Artist as a Young Man,*[41] or in Winterson's *Oranges are Not the Only Fruit.*[42] Such preaching and teaching plays upon and abuses the 'fear' and 'self-interest' motivations for moral behaviour, that Kohlberg has identified as the basis of the first two stages (and the first level) of his model of moral development. Furthermore, if images and metaphors are always put across as if they are literally true and as if they are unquestionable, or if they are conveyed as ends in themselves, children and adults are prevented from developing more mature attitudes to faith and belief, especially if they do not understand that they are permitted, if they wish, to give up the images of their childhood. They are so tied to them that they never grow out of fantasy to ask the questions evoked by the realities of life in the world.

Images, symbols and stories clearly matter greatly as ways of learning to play with and experience the world. For children, they are glimpses (albeit sometimes exaggerated in their goodness and their wickedness) of the world of adults for which they are being prepared in their long period of dependence. Bettelheim observes that fairy stories (and religious stories — he sees little difference in their themes and purpose) 'come to speak simultaneously to all levels of the human personality, communicating in a manner which reaches the uneducated mind of the child as well as that of the sophisticated adult'.[43]

The parallel between the fairy story and the Bible story is an interesting one, since in the Christian tradition (though I think not within the Hindu tradition, and certainly not in Buddhism) many stories are told as if what is central to them is their historical truth rather than their psychological truth. Bettelheim describes the value of the fairy tale as 'the child . . . can swing back and forth in his own mind between "It's true, that's how one acts and reacts" and "It's all untrue, it's just a story"'.[44] Children do not appear to get to a stage with fairy stories when they feel let down and disappointed or deceived because the story is not true (although they do sometimes over Father Christmas, which raises questions, that I cannot examine here, about the significance of that particular character). It is unfortunate that many of the symbols of religion (at least in the West) are put across and perceived in such a way as to lead many people to disillusionment (in a negative sense) and to loss of confidence in the churches who use them. People 'see through' them and 'do not believe in them', whereas there was nothing to believe in them in the first place. Symbols should point beyond themselves, but all too often in the case of the churches they have been made to point to disputed historical facts and theological ideas, rather than to indisputable aspects of human experience. Those who reject religious symbols do not 'see through them' to other truths beyond, but see through them in the sense of having been deceived about their true meaning. They no longer trust that there is anything of value in them. 'Seeing through' images, as I have described here, is in fact a more advanced level of belief which means looking beyond them, rather than being disappointed at the dawning realization that a symbol is nothing in itself. Meanwhile, the secular symbols of everyday life (for example, as used in advertising) replace the symbols of religion and continue to attract, bemuse, and please, even though many people can see through them too.

Stories need to be told, as fairy stories are themselves, for their underlying truths (which will be different for every one who hears them) more than for their factual reality. If they are related in that way, adults may be able to go on loving and using the religious and non-religious stories that they have learned as children, without having to strain their credulity or their confidence in the integrity of their belief. The 'as if' quality which psychoanalysis has identified as a valuable way of relating to a therapist, since it draws out many of the issues which most deeply affect clients, is equally important in the use of language and symbols, particularly in relation to religion, literature and the arts. Adults may be helped to 'see through' images, symbols and metaphors to deeper meanings, when they have been convinced that it is not necessary to take them literally.

Yet, at this point in this study, I anticipate developments that may become possible later in life for some people in their journey of belief. For the time being, in order to take the reader into the mythic-literal Stage which forms part of the next developmental theme, it is valuable to summarize Stage 1 as a world full of symbols, some of which may be 'religious', some of which may be from other sources, and some of which come from other aspects of the prevailing culture. In the very early months of life, symbols are pre-verbal (indeed closely identified with transitional objects), but as the child grows and hears stories, and develops stories in her or his own imagination, she is involved in attempts to make sense of conflicting and sometimes anxiety-provoking experiences, by using the powerful imagery of fantasy. In many respects, it is a delightful stage, when everything and anything can be believed, no matter how contradictory the different ideas in a child's mind may appear to an adult. It is the images that capture the imagination, and not any specific message that an adult might wish to attach to them. It is a stage which William James, affectionately quoted by Fowler, called 'blooming, buzzing confusion'!

The responsibility of the adult

The study of hospital patients' views of God, to which I referred earlier, found that the images of God which the patients had were more influenced by their actual parents than by formal religious instruction. The authors of the study believe that by the time a child is introduced to formal religious teaching, the image of God is fixed and difficult to re-shape.[45] This is a bold conclusion, and one which appears to question the possibility of change, whether through education, through psychotherapy and counselling, or even through alternative spiritual experiences. The question of whether people are able to make significant changes in a new environment and in the context of a caring relationship tends to become an article of belief in itself. It has divided Freudians and person-centred therapists, pessimists and optimists, the *angst* of Europe and the brash hope of the United States. The ability to change is a long-debated theological question as well, setting predestination and free-will against each other. Are people condemned to be dogged by negative experiences, or blessed with the assurance of life-long positive favours?

There is some support for what appears an almost deterministic position in Winnicott, although he expresses it with a different emphasis. Like the authors of the study of hospital patients, he feels that it was not in Sunday Schools or churches that children first learned about faith. In a lecture about the way children learn, he said: 'We are believing people because we were started off well by somebody. We received a silent communication over a long period of time that we were loved in the sense that we could rely on the environmental provision and so get on with our *own* growth and development' (my italics).[46]

Winnicott, whose positive view of illusion must now be becoming familiar to the reader, is again particularly relevant here. Among the many evocative catch-phrases which have been adopted from Winnicott's work, is the expression 'the facilitating environment' — an essential provision for healthy development. This includes 'being with' and providing a safe, 'holding' presence, and he suggests that, through this, children (and adults) learn more about ultimate qualities such as faith, hope and love. Such qualities are not learned through teaching or preaching. Only 'on the basis of what has been experienced by an individual', Winnicott said in the lecture already cited, '[can we] teach the concept of, say, the everlasting arms'.

Although he was brought up as a Methodist, Winnicott was not speaking about the value of religion, but about the value of early mothering. Speaking on a different occasion, he was more critical of religion, and suggested an alternative to the communication of faith and moral sense by the teaching of religion, whether by brute force, or by more subtle means. 'The good alternative has to do with the provision of those conditions for the infant and child that enable such things as trust and "belief in", and ideas of right and wrong, to develop out of the working of the individual child's inner processes.'[47] Given a start in life which involves being cared for in a reliable way, 'the idea of goodness and of a reliable and personal parent or God can follow naturally'.[48]

Winnicott once commented upon his Wesleyan, Methodist origins, 'I am always glad that my religious upbringing was of a kind that allowed for growing up out of'.[49] This point on the journey of belief is one which I shall not come to until after looking at more conventional attitudes in the next chapter, although Winnicott reminds us that the ability to 'grow up out of' is fostered in the early stages of development, by developing a particular type of trust and a particular type of dependency. It is one which allows for disillusionment, the second major task of the nursing mother which follows helping to create illusion. The sort of disillusionment that is positive in its process and in its outcome enables illusions to be given up, without destroying the basic capacity to believe. It is the sense of belief, coupled with another quality which Erikson identifies with the first Age—hope—that enables people to go on to ask questions and to create more illusions for themselves. Disillusionment in the positive sense leads not to cynicism and despair, but to what might be described (to use deliberately another oral stage image) as a 'thirst for knowledge'.

Although he is conversant with psychoanalysis, Cupitt does not demonstrate any obvious knowledge of Winnicott's work. Perhaps therefore independently, he has also identified that in the stage of trust and dependency a baby has to learn how to tolerate separateness from mother. Cupitt suggests that, since the mother 'is not around all or much of the time, [the baby] must eventually frame some kind of world-hypothesis which postulates her identity and continuity between her appearances. This may be connected with faith in the power of the Word, i.e. how reliably she appears when he yells'.[50] This is a neat pun on the significance of 'the Word', which lends support to the substance of this chapter: that it is in the early mothering experience that world-views are first formed.

It appears that some world-views remain unchanged throughout life, providing a way of tolerating, appreciating and ordering different life events. Where these world-views or patterns of belief remain at the simplest levels described in this chapter, they can take an optimistic or a pessimistic form—either form may help their proponents to accommodate or integrate their experience. In other people, world-views develop further; at the next stage normally in a conventional context, even if later there may be radical changes of belief and of loyalties. In the course of this next stage development, 'the Word' tends to become expressed (some might even say 'lost') in many other words, as ordering the many varieties of inner experience and the welter of external stimuli becomes the most pressing need. This urgent task is a necessary one nonetheless, since it extends the possibilities of belief which subsequent chapters will address.

Notes

1. M. Jacobs, *Towards the Fullness of Christ* (London: Darton, Longman and Todd, 1988), p. 40.
2. S. Freud, *Postscript to 'The Question of Lay Analysis'* (London: Penguin Freud Library), vol. 15, p. 358.
3. Matthew 18. 2–6.
4. Ephesians 1. 5.
5. Ephesians 5. 1.
6. 1 Corinthians 13. 11.
7. Ephesians 4. 14.
8. 1 Corinthians 14. 20.
9. C. Dickens, *Hard Times* (1854), chapter 2.
10. W. E. Baldridge and J. J. Gleason, 'A Theological Framework for Pastoral Care', *Journal of Pastoral Care*, 32:4 (1978), p. 237.
11. D. W. Winnicott, *Collected Papers: Through Paediatrics to Psychoanalysis* (London: Hogarth Press, 1975), p. 153.
12. S. Freud, *The Future of an Illusion* (London: Penguin Freud Library), vol. 12, p. 212.
13. J. London, *White Fang* (New York: Dover Publications, 1991), p. 59. Originally published by Macmillan in 1906.
14. S. Freud, *Totem and Taboo* (London: Penguin Freud Library), vol. 13.
15. J. W. Fowler, *Stages of Faith: the Psychology of Human Development and the Quest for Meaning* (San Francisco: Harper and Row, 1981), p. 121.
16. H. Faber, *Psychology of Religion* (London: SCM Press, 1976).
17. W. G. Justice and W. Lambert, 'A Comparative Study of the Language People Use to Describe the Personalities of God and their Earthly Parents', *Journal of Pastoral Care*, 40:2 (1986), pp. 166–72.
18. Winnicott, *Collected Papers*, p. 201.
19. M. Balint, *The Basic Fault* (Tavistock Publications, 1968), p. 72.
20. D. Zohar, *The Quantum Self* (London: HarperCollins, 1991), p. 123.
21. See a particularly useful summary of arguments for, and images of, the motherhood of God in S. McFague, *Models of God* (London: Fortress Press and SCM Press, 1987), chapter 4, 'God as Mother'. *See also* K. Leech, *True God* (London: Sheldon Press, 1985), chapter 12, 'God the Mother'; and A. Loades, *Searching for Lost Coins* (London: SPCK, 1987), chapter 5, 'God and god-ess'.
22. *Julian of Norwich: Showings* tr. E. Colledge and J. Walsh (Paulist Press and SPCK, 1978), chapter 59. For a summary *see* J. Gatta, *A Pastoral Art* (London: Darton, Longman and Todd, 1987), pp. 71–4.
23. E. Erikson, *Young Man Luther* (London: Faber & Faber, 1959), p. 257.

24. S. Freud, *Obsessive Actions and Religious Practices* (London: Penguin Freud Library), vol. 13, pp. 31–41.
25. Winnicott, *Collected Papers*, p. 242.
26. Genesis 3. 24.
27. I. Shah, *The Way of the Sufi* (London: Penguin Books, 1974), p. 26.
28. Shah, p. 33.
29. A. Watts, *The Spirit of Zen* (London, HarperCollins, 1991), p. 20.
30. D. E. Harding, *On Having No Head* (London and New York: Arkana, 1986), p. 25.
31. E. Fromm, *The Greatness and Limitations of Freud's Thought* (London: Jonathan Cape, 1980), p. 132.
32. Luke 16. 20–4.
33. Faber, p. 160.
34. Faber, p. 168.
35. Justice and Lambert, p. 166.
36. Faber, pp. 148–9.
37. Baldridge and Gleason, p. 232.
38. R. C. Zaehner, *Hinduism* (Oxford University Press, 1962), p. 85.
39. Winnicott, *Collected Papers*, p. 233.
40. J. R. R. Tolkien, *Tree and Leaf* (London: Unwin Books, 1964), p. 66.
41. J. Joyce, *A Portrait of the Artist as a Young Man* (London: Jonathan Cape, 1916), chapter 3.
42. J. Winterson, *Oranges are Not the Only Fruit* (London: Bloomsbury Publishing, 1991).
43. B. Bettelheim, *The Uses of Enchantment* (London: Penguin Books, 1978), pp. 5–6.
44. Bettelheim, p. 31.
45. *See also* A.-M. Rizzuto, *The Birth of the Living God* (University of Chicago Press, 1979).
46. D. W. Winnicott, *Home is Where We Start From* (London: Penguin Books, 1986), pp. 141–50.
47. D. W. Winnicott, *The Maturational Processes and the Facilitating Environment* (London: Hogarth Press, 1965), p. 94.
48. Winnicott, *The Maturational Processes and the Facilitating Environment*, p. 97.
49. Winnicott, *Home is Where We Start From*, p. 142.
50. D. Cupitt, *Life Lines* (London: SCM Press, 1986), p. 18.

FOUR

Authority and Autonomy

═══════

Getting it together

Following the 'blooming and buzzing confusion' that William James describes as the age of infancy, the next period of personal development consists of learning to impose a type of order upon experience. The term 'anal' refers, among other things, to the ability a child acquires (because of increased control of the sphincter muscles) to urinate and defecate 'to order' rather than accidentally. The term disguises the fact that sphincter and bladder control is only one of many aspects of muscular development which enable a child to begin to learn to co-ordinate brain and body, in walking, handling, dismantling, putting together, building, self-feeding, and so on. In a physical sense, a child begins to get things together.

This is reflected in language development, where the speech muscles gradually become strong enough to form definite sounds and words; and it is also reflected in the child's growing capacity to understand what she hears from adults and older children. Great changes in an infant's capabilities take place throughout childhood, but perhaps these take place most quickly during the years after the first and second birthdays. It is almost as if a child had been waiting to acquire the physical strength to do new things, because the spurts in activity that take place are enormous, once the first steps are taken, once the hands begin to manipulate objects and once the first words are learned.

Yet, this physical ability to co-ordinate also reflects a psychological wish to make order out of the potential chaos of so many new experiences. In this task, a child recognizes the help that adults can give, since they have skills and knowledge to pass on to a child to help her learn how to deal with all the stimuli which the expanding world provides. Adults provide an authority, which, in the end, can develop and encourage a child or a young person in becoming her own authority — to become autonomous.

Another word that summarizes much of this level of development and belief is 'control'. Controlling oneself, controlling experience, controlling ideas and thought, and to some extent controlling one's environment, are all major issues. Autonomy also gives rise to problems of how far other people's control (like parental authority) has to be accepted, and how much it can be questioned. The term 'convention' means 'coming together', and it is in such a positive sense that this age is important; it also means convention in the sense of unthinking conformity. The danger of this age is the suppression of autonomy. The weakness of forms of belief which are associated with this latter part of this period of personal development is that they become conformist and conventional, instead of providing the basis for greater independence of thought and belief.

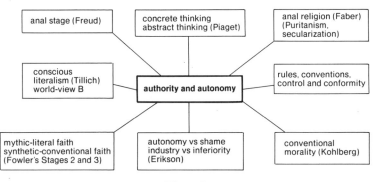

Figure 8

To help order the different models, which otherwise might confuse a psychology of personal development and belief, I cluster in Figure 8 the various terms and stages which link personal growth with changes in ways of perceiving and thinking, and so open up further patterns for this chapter to examine.

Although this may appear to be the middle theme of the three which I use to describe forms of faith and belief, and therefore in some sense a transitional one, it is one which is also for many people an end in itself. This is particularly true of many examples of religious faith, although it also applies in the case of other expressions of knowledge and belief. 'Authority' is extremely powerful, whether it takes the form of parents, experts, facts or theories—and achieving autonomy is much less common than we like to think. If anything, there is more openness to the varieties of experience at the first level of belief than there is in this one—although this second level contains the possibility of providing a rich treasury of thought and tradition, upon which those who function at the third level often draw in turn.

As a child's body develops, and as the muscles begin to respond better to the child's own wishes, there is a growing sense of control and co-ordination. What concerns us more in this chapter is a continuing movement to control and order experience and knowledge, something which (as I have shown in the last chapter) had already started in infancy. There is a type of ordering of experience when a baby tries to make sense of the difference between its chaotic 'world' where she is fed one moment and hungry another, or is alone at one time and held close at another. She orders such bewilderment through fantasies (that may seem strange to adults) of a good and a bad breast. Such ordering serves to make transitional sense of the whole bewildering business. With the development of thinking and of language, there comes both the wish to know (what some have called a drive for knowledge) and the desire to make some sense of sensations, of words, of other people's behaviour and of parental rules. The questioning child wants to get it straight, to order, to understand and to 'get things taped'. Initially, the means to this is replete with symbolism and fantasy.

In relating the stages of different models, I played with the idea of placing Fowler's Stage 2, 'mythic-literal faith' with the first set of 'trust and dependency' themes. In fact, I have already done as much in describing forms of belief which are strongly reliant upon myth and story. It may be deceptive to think of the more 'simple' kind of faith described in the last chapter as purely Fowler's Stage 1, since it is more a blend of Stages 1 and 2. Moving out of the 'blooming, buzzing confusion' of symbols and images already present in the first separate Stage of faith development, Fowler suggests that Stage 2 consists of the bringing together of symbols into more continuous stories and myths.[1] It is this collating, collecting and pulling together which weighed in favour of my inclusion of Fowler's Stage 2 in a set of themes, where this sense of ordering ties up with 'anal stage' issues.

I have in mind children who are older than the toddler age, although I do not forget that there is a strong wish to know 'why the sky is blue' and 'what clouds are made of' even at that earlier age. The wish to order experience and to make sense of it leads children who are even older than two or three to force what they hear and experience into a mind-set with which they are already familiar. Phrases used in religious terminology, because they are often framed in old-fashioned or in abstract language, provide particularly good examples of the need to order, although spell-check programmes on personal computers illustrate just as well how, with a limited vocabulary, both a child and an Apple Macintosh can come up with bizarre alternatives. Thus, when spell-checking this chapter, my word processor threw up Cupid as the suggested spelling for Cupitt, Paint for Piaget and Toilet as the suggested spelling for Tillich. In one way, my computer's information base is like a child's in its limitations, because it can only go to words it knows, and cannot admit that it is ignorant (unless it finds nothing similar at all). From the religious context, there are examples of phrases in the Lord's Prayer that show how children often turn what they are told or hear into a form which they can understand: 'Lead us not into Thames station', 'Vikings will come' and 'Harold be thy name' are all examples I have come across, all of which are rather sensible variations on the more familiar archaic phrases adults use. The last phrase suggests an even longer explanation: one woman remembered thinking as a child that 'Harold' ('hallowed' in the Lord's Prayer) was the Harold who was their church gardener and that, in church, they were praying to him. Harold the gardener made more sense to her as an eight-year-old than an unseen unknown God. This strong compulsion to make sense of what we see and hear, is the basis of the projection tests which psychologists use. Even an ink-blot assumes clearer shapes when we are asked to associate to it. Children can get very frightened by patterns on wallpaper at night, when they see faces or fantastic animals that do not go away once spotted. Anxiety at not knowing, and at not understanding, and other internal anxieties can push people into premature ways of ordering provocative and evocative stimuli.

Much the same need to make sense of the incomprehensible leads children to misunderstand some aspects of adult rules and behaviour. Such rules are not as logical and consistent to a child as they appear to a parent, who has come to understand the subtleties of what can be done, as well as where, when and by whom. In one sense, the old books of etiquette may be outdated, but there are just as many family and social conventions as ever appeared in one of those manuals. Since children have only a limited number of ways of looking at issues, they often find it difficult to discriminate between the nuances of adult rules and behaviour. The expression, 'Don't do as I do, do as I say,' may well be how a child experiences the difference between a parent's injunctions and the example set by adults, even if the older generation do not intend to convey such a message. The rules parents impart to their children are inevitably simplifications of complex adult conventions. Hence the misunderstandings that lead to phrases such as, 'But you told me I had to . . .', and the reply, 'But I didn't mean that!' Needless to say, such examples of non-comprehension occur at other levels of discourse in adult to adult conversations: differences of beliefs and values between adults are just as difficult to convey to those who have not yet experienced (or do not remember) what the other is talking about. Grown men and women can find it equally difficult to tolerate the nuances involved in intellectual and moral thinking or in systems of belief.

From an early age, therefore, a child is involved in an immense task of learning about the external world. Children soak up knowledge as they grow older. They often possess more information about certain favourite topics than most adults do. They can handle sophisticated games (such as computer games or puzzles) which require complex mental and physical co-ordination—again often much better than many adults. Small wonder then that a child works just as hard at sorting out the messages that are attached to stories, to folk tales, to religion, and other areas of learning which are not as logical as basic adding up and taking away. Images and symbols may in themselves be used to find some sense of meaning, although more commonly in the age of cognitive development which concerns us here, it is the whole story that matters. This is the age when it is difficult for an adult to omit or change any of the details of a story without being told to 'tell it properly'. There is as yet no stepping back from the story to reflect upon it, nor any wish to have the same meaning communicated in more abstract terms. Meaning can only be experienced through the concrete. Fowler suggests that 'meaning is both carried and "trapped" in the narrative', although the term 'trapped' itself seems a strangely limited way of looking at a child's experience of stories, which is often far richer than that of many adults, even if the richness of the child's experience can never adequately be put into words.[2]

In Fowler's Stage 2, the symbols and images which dominated the earlier 'intuitive-projective' Stage begin to take on more definite shape, as stories are assembled from them and the images themselves are refined. He gives some useful examples of this development by citing how descriptions of God change as children move from Stage 1 to Stage 2. He calls this a change from nascent to more developed anthromorphic images. Freddy is a child who is identified as demonstrating Stage 1 thinking. When Freddy is asked the question, 'What is God like?', he answers: 'He has a light shirt on, brown hair and brown eyelashes'.[3] There is nothing special about this description, and it is a simple projection on to God of the picture of a very ordinary man. It appears that Freddy says the first thing that comes into his head. The description might even match that of the interviewer who is talking to Freddy. The researcher provides a convenient description for Freddy to give, which quickly reduces the little boy's anxiety at not knowing the answer to such an impossible question.

Such a question may in one sense not seem fair—how could we expect a child to answer it when adults cannot? The point is that many adults would not attempt to answer it by giving a *physical* description—it is not a question which can be answered that way. In fact, the question itself is no more obscure than some of those which children ask adults, even if they are often content with the unhelpful answer 'because they do', or 'because they are'! What Fowler's research shows (and Goldman's, *see* page 29) is that beliefs about areas of experience, which are not capable of being described in *concrete* terms at this stage, take a variety of forms. They draw on the concrete in order to express the inexpressible. Children try to make sense of their experience, and of the questions they are asked or which they ask themselves; but they are not yet disturbed that their answers may be wrong, illogical or inconsistent. Later, particularly as adolescents or young adults, they can be troubled by this, and they may then move into Stage 3 thinking.

Freddy's answer is imaginative, and even if he says probably the first thing that comes into his head, this is typical of the 'intuitive-projective' Stage in which he is. When Millie is asked the same question, 'What is God like?', she gives an answer which is indicative of Stage 2 (the 'mythic-literal' Stage). She describes God in much more conventional terms, perhaps influenced by the traditional pictures conveyed to her by parents, by the churches, by other adults and by television (in her case). But there is clear evidence that she is thinking more deeply about what she is saying, because she prefaces her description by saying she does not *know* the answer, and she knows she is imagining: 'I don't know. But . . . I imagine that he's an old man with a white beard and white hair wearing a long robe, and that the clouds are his floor and he has a throne, and he has all these people and there's angels around him . . . he has a nice face and blue eyes . . . and he's forgiving.'[4]

This is a more developed set of images. God is still described as a man, but Millie's other answers reveal that her picture of God is much more than what he *looks* like. God is also given some personal qualities, such as being 'forgiving'. Her description goes on to indicate that Millie believes that he makes mistakes, like her parents do, revealing again how close the parental projection is in many pictures of God's qualities. Despite an apparently simple faith, there are signs of growing puzzlement in Millie's Stage 2 understanding. Concrete thinking is beginning to reveal its weaknesses for her, and it does not answer all her questions.

Again, Freddy (in Stage 1) is asked how God, whom Freddy sees as a man, can be everywhere. Without any sense of contradiction or tautology, Freddy answers that 'he can split up or he can be like God'.[5] In an example in Goldman's earlier research, nine-year-old Peter (who might be at the equivalent point of Fowler's Stage 2) cannot reconcile how

God can be in one place, the Burning Bush, and yet be everywhere at the same time. Goldman comments: 'He evinces a great deal of confusion about these scripture stories, being unable to transcend their concrete imagery and language, and as a result accepts them at a literal level, although plainly dissatisfied with his explanation . . . He solves these and other problems mainly by ignoring them and by beginning to separate "the religious" from the rest of experience'.[6] The last phrase is a disturbingly accurate comment on what happens to the religious belief of many people who begin to question. It is separated from the rest of experience, and relegated to a dark corner. My argument throughout this book is that religious belief should not be regarded as different from any other form of belief. There must be room for questioning, and for Stage 3 logical explanation (or lack of it), but there must also be encouragement to move beyond the limits of the concrete, the conventional and the factual to other ways of believing as well.

There is a literalism in Fowler's description of Stage 2 as 'mythic-literal' which links it to Stage 1; but there is also a growing sense of order. The present stage of belief which I am considering, a mixture of myths and stories, of relatively straightforward trust in simple rules (of logic and language as well as behaviour) is on the edge of Tillich's world-view A, a stage of natural or pre-conscious literalism. It is beginning to move, as Millie's and Peter's questioning shows, into world-view B, where other questions need to be addressed. Tillich's description captures the way this position is right on the edge of world-view A, because it is 'still justifiable if the questioning power is very weak and can easily be answered'.[7] It is interesting, taking a different perspective, to see how in his 'Metro-map' of the development of theological thinking Cupitt identifies one of the earliest stages as a type of thinking which he calls 'mythical realism'. His description of mythical realism as a system of thought is remarkably similar to Goldman's and Fowler's descriptions about an individual's level of belief. Although mythical realism is pictorial and appears unsystematic, this is only when it is judged by later standards. Cupitt writes: 'Concern for the systematic organization of the self, of society, of the world, of life and time and of the religious realm itself is by no means absent. But it is still relatively weak, because the need for it has not yet been deeply felt'.[8] He contrasts this with doctrinal realism, with all the rigour of distinct beliefs and organization, which I come to below as the equivalent of Fowler's Stage 3. In the next stage of the development of belief, attempts are made to provide answers for some of the important questions that are raised about faith and facts, even if these questions can seem strangely inappropriate or incomplete (from the point of view of even later development). The mistake that those in positions of authority often make (and it is they who are approached as the 'adult' experts) is to try to allay the anxiety behind the questioning. They provide answers that appear to override the contradictions that arise inevitably from the juxtaposition of myths and stories with the 'hard' evidence of the material world and factual disciplines. The rich and varied resources of myth, fairy tale, religious story, image and symbol or primitive explanation get lost in the desire for rational explanation and logical consistency. Only in children is such 'un-thinking' tolerated (often condescendingly) as being 'sweet' or 'cute'. The difficulty of moving into the next stage of faith development is how to move into more rational discourse, without losing all the 'magic' of all that has gone before, and without becoming so 'conventional' that other avenues of perception are closed off.

Conventional reality

There is much that is vital about learning conventions and rules. Growing up, for example, may involve what Winnicott calls 'growing up *out of*', but it also involves growing up *into* a family, a community and a society. Unconventional and non-conformist though he was as a psychoanalyst, Winnicott also believes that it takes ten years before a new analyst is ready to move out of his or her training.[9] In learning any new discipline, it is necessary to learn the rules, the conventions and the traditional knowledge (if only to avoid re-inventing the wheel), before even considering developing new ways of working within the discipline.

Similarly, the boundaries of an infant, living to begin with in a tiny 'world' that is easily confused with the rudimentary self, have to extend into a wider world that also consists of the expectations, wishes and conventions of other people. Children need to learn to accommodate their wishes and demands to what others feel and can provide: a process which brings pleasure and satisfaction at times, but frustration and disapproval at others. Life in a family, a community and society at large, as much as in any professional society, guild or trade in adult life, involves learning not just the folk-lore (the stories and images which are particularly important in Fowler's Stage 2), but also folk-law, the rules and codes of behaviour which govern family and community life (Fowler's Stage 3 and Kohlberg's conventional level of moral thinking). This learning includes moral, religious and 'society' rules, many of which are not so clearly stated, but are individual, family and community interpretations of right and wrong. Learning to live with others involves learning the conventional rewards and punishments that attend conforming to or rejecting those people's expectations. If children find it difficult to understand reasons for some of the ways they should or should not behave, they understand with ease the pleasure and displeasure of adults. Fear and bargaining (Kohlberg's first two stages of moral development) give way to conformity and the wish to please others, to gain their approval (Kohlberg's third and fourth stages).

In a variety of ways, growing children need to learn how to deal with (and how they are *meant* to deal with) the realities of the external world around them. Indeed, this might be called the age of reality—or this particular form of belief might be called reality thinking. However, it is important to recognize (in a way which strict rationalists or logical positivist philosophers do not) that even reality thinking itself, and the belief in the supremacy of reason, is another of the illusions through which we live our lives. Freud gives reality the title 'the reality-principle', although I suspect he did not recognize that it too has illusory qualities. Despite the high value he attaches to the messages of the illusions that come through dreams, day-dreams, fantasies and their expression in art and literature, Freud's rationalism sets up the reality principle as end in itself.[10] He recognized, perhaps more clearly than anyone of his time, our capacity for self-deception, but there always remained for him the possibility of the desired goal of freedom from illusion through reality testing.

In children, Freud maintains, the pleasure-principle holds sway: 'pleasure' in the sense he uses it means both achieving pleasure and satisfaction (such as the enjoyment of being fed, or the warmth and comfort of mother's arms), as well as the relief of tension (as in defecation or through the relief of hunger). But it is essential to move towards the reality principle to live in an adult world, and to survive the dangers and deprivations of external reality. Freud's view of adult life is (in one sense correctly) a sober and pessimistic one, although it is relieved at times by references to the imaginative and creative world of art and literature, that demonstrate his recognition of other ways of perceiving reality. I return in the next chapter to this important corrective to Freud's otherwise rather narrow reality-principle.

Realistic thinking and reality-testing in Freud's model of development is reflected in a number of ways in other disciplines. In the development of art, for example, realism became a major force during the Renaissance (although as far as sculpture is concerned, such realism marked a *rediscovery* of classical form). In painting especially, the use of perspective made for realistic portrayal of people and places. This is completely in line with the theme of this chapter, and as Clark observes: 'The belief that one could represent a man in a *real* setting and *calculate* his position and *arrange* figures in a demonstrably harmonious *order*, expressed symbolically a new idea about man's *place* in the scheme of things and man's *control* over his own destiny'.[11] The italics are mine, and show how closely his description of the Renaissance reflects some of the terms which accompany the 'anal' stage of control and autonomy.

As might be expected of that great flowering of the tree of knowledge, the Renaissance also gave rise to huge advances in science, particularly in the one hundred year period from Bacon through to Halley which has been called the Age of Newton. Indeed, Freud bridges the end of this particular rationalist tradition in science and the first signs of new principles of scientific thinking, in what might be called the Age of Einstein. Capra outlines classical physics as:

[A] mechanistic view of nature . . . closely related to rigorous determinism. The giant cosmic machine was seen as being completely causal and determinate. All that happened had a definite cause and gave rise to definite effect, and the future of any part of the system could—in principle—be predicted with absolute certainty . . .[12]

Capra also observes that, in the course of its development, classical physics (i.e. in the context of Greek philosophy) lost touch with the spiritual, leading to a split between the 'spiritual world' and the 'material world'. For the first 1500 years of Christendom, the emphasis was (sometimes in a heavily materialistic form) on the spiritual. With the Renaissance, the emphasis changed to the humanistic and the materialistic. It is this same split which is often reflected in the clear dichotomy between art and science, or religion and science; examined, for example in C. P. Snow's *The Two Cultures*.[13] Capra adds that Descartes' view of nature, as fundamentally divided into two independent realms of mind and matter, has perpetuated the temptation for science to treat matter as dead, and under the control of scientists.[14] I want to add that there is a temptation in every discipline to treat its subject (whether it be the natural world, Shakespeare or God) as in some way inanimate, and virtually under its own control. Perhaps the ultimate of this is the use of computers in creating what is grandiosely called 'virtual reality'.

The centrality of realism is seen also in Cupitt's analysis of the development of theological thought in his 'Metro-map', where he identifies what he calls doctrinal realism and metaphysical realism.[15] In brief, religious thinking of this type takes the form of an ordered system, which is seen in the setting out of beliefs in authoritatively stated and ordered creeds or in the need for ordered sequences, found in various world faiths in the five pillars of faith, the ten commandments or the eight-fold path. The passion for order leads to attempts to rationalize some of the apparent contradictions; for example, the Christian church arrives at the Trinitarian formula of three persons in one God, or the two natures of Christ, wholly man and wholly God. The wish for order, in churches and in society, has also led to a hierarchical system: a pyramid-like structure, which reflects the theological idea of orders of being. This is also present in the caste system in Hinduism.

In no sense do I wish to devalue the importance of reality, the necessity of the reality-principle or the process of communication of tradition. In joining any community (whether sacred or secular, intellectual or political), and in embarking upon a more thorough understanding of any subject, it is necessary to learn its conventions gradually, in order to share in the accumulated wisdom of the community (as I have already indicated). This not only helps the community to accept a new member, but provides the new member with the raw materials from which more individual development can take place in due course. An analogy to this is the equal need, at a certain stage of their development, to help children learn to read and write, and to acquire both basic information and simple logic, if they are to gain deeper knowledge in their later studies. Such learning forms the basis from which they can go on into abstract thinking (to follow Piaget's model of cognitive development), and which they can apply in their studies in further or higher education. At the right time, children also learn how to frame questions, how to weigh and balance evidence, and how they can generate new ideas and fresh interpretations. To use Fowler's faith development terminology, 'synthetic-conventional faith' has considerable importance, even if the implication of his model is that the path towards maturity should lead further to the 'individuative-reflective' Stage.[16]

Fowler uses 'synthetic' in the sense of drawing upon other people's ways of thinking, although not in the sense that an individual at this point tries to create her or his own synthesis. Fowler describes this type of faith as 'conventional', although this is not a derogatory term. He recognizes that such faith takes account of a wider world and wider issues, and provides a coherent orientation in the midst of the complexities of life. It provides a sense of identity and outlook, although it is more a sense of common identity—just as an adolescent finds security in his or her own sub-culture. There is as yet no real sense of autonomous judgement. In some ways, Fowler suggests, it is more like an ideology than a personal faith, even though the beliefs may be very deeply held.[17] Authority is still vested in traditional authority figures or in the valued peer group.

The parallel with adolescence is useful here, although the rarer, deeply radical type of adolescent thinking features in the next chapter. During adolescence, two factors normally influence the questioning of rules and experimentation with alternative modes of behaviour. Firstly young people, as part of their quest for independence, need to test out and challenge the authority of their parents and of those who exercise control over them. In this respect, battles of will are little different from early childhood, except that the young man or woman has more weight. By this I mean not just physical strength, but also greater weight in their power of argument. Young people use to the full their new-found ability to play with concepts, and to back up their arguments with abstract thinking, such as Piaget suggests becomes possible just before puberty. This playing with (or twisting) words is partly what makes it more difficult to argue with young people, and with people in Stage 3 of any belief development.

The second factor in their questioning is the need to find a set of rules for themselves, accepted not because others say so, but because they recognize that certain rules, conventions or ideas have validity after all. Out of this period of experimentation, which is sometimes only in mental or verbal argument, although sometimes also in activity too, a maturing young person begins to discover something of her or his own identity, and the beginnings of a more personal set of values and ideas of what is right and wrong. They also begin to identify what is important and what is peripheral in the body of tradition that has been taught them by word and example since their childhood. These values and ideas are not necessarily any different in content to parental and community standards (indeed they are often the same). They are only different because they are now based upon self-discovery, rather than upon the need to conform to or rebel against the wishes of others. This is Kohlberg's fourth stage of moral development (which runs parallel to the finding of a personal identity in the Erikson model), that of personal recognition of the value of moral laws and social order.

This questioning takes people from 'mythic-literal' forms of belief into the 'synthetic-conventional' Stage, although this type of faith is different again from the more radical questioning of the next Stage, which I describe more fully in the next chapter. Many adolescents are in fact heavily conformist, and conventional, particularly influenced by their peer group and by a youth sub-culture, to which they often slavishly adhere. Finding an individual identity, in the true sense of becoming an individual, normally comes much later if it comes at all. We have a mistaken idea that adolescence is the sole time of identity formation. More idiosyncratic and personal views tend to come later, after sharing for a considerable time in a common identity.

Not only adolescents, but many adults as well, are notoriously conformist, whether in their moral thinking, in their social expectations or in their attitudes to religious faith, politics or intellectual opinion. It is this conventional type of belief, the 'synthetic-conventional' Stage, which Fowler identifies in people of all kinds as the most common form of religious faith. I suspect that this is also true of other expressions of belief. Fowler believes that the majority of people in religious groups belong to this category.[18] But he also identifies the majority of those who are not committed to religion, and indeed critical of it, as showing the same 'synthetic-conventional' characteristics. Many of those who hold anti-religious or non-religious views (except perhaps in a crisis, when they sometimes return or regress to religion), express their ideas in a very conventional way. When they pass opinions, they often say more about their conformity to cultural norms than about their own understanding of faith or of other forms of belief.

As an example, Fowler quotes a middle-aged man, whose attitude appears to be that things are and always have been the same, and who gives the impression of being 'stuck' in his views. When he talks about religious faith, the man is no different:

> I'm not now a religious man, never was and never will be. Religion is just a lot of nonsense as I see it. As I see it, we are born, we live here, we die, and that's it. Religion gives people something to believe in, that there's something more, because they want there to be something more, but there isn't.[19]

A statement such as this, merely printed on the page, lacks accompanying expression. Some of these ideas might have been thought out and, expressed rather differently, could have suggested a more 'individuative-reflective' view. But the example is an attempt to convey the type of attitude that draws on conventional, popular wisdom and is believed to be 'common sense'. There is a certain dogmatism about the sentiments which might just as easily have appeared in a religious person. It is very hard for people to break away from dominant cultural assumptions and become their own judge and interpreter; to hold opinions, which are not just intellectually true for them, but which are also emotionally and intuitively valid.

Ironically, although faith at this stage is sometimes blinkered and single-minded, it is far from simple or narrow. The need to answer the questions which arise at this point often gives rise to a vast amount of opinion and knowledge. There are many books that deal with the conventions and traditions of every type of discipline. Whether it is religious faith or scientific beliefs that we are concerned about, the amount of detail, the facts and the figures, and the multiplicity of theories all testify to the productivity of this mode of belief. Indeed, numbers of words may be more indicative of this stage, since in other stages myth, metaphor, poetry, music and art convey meaning more concisely in a different, less verbose form.

Nor in religious terms does this period of 'synthetic-conventional faith' question the sincerity with which people may believe, or the depth of their experience of God — and 'God' it normally is, since the value and attraction of less precise terms such as 'the transcendent' is not yet relevant. Belief in God may involve a deep sense of *personal* relationship with the divine. The *personal qualities* of God become more important as the attributes of physical imagery no longer hold. Questioning may be consistent and thorough, and the answers increasingly complex, as people explore their belief systems, whether about religion, science or any other form of discourse. The need for a clear sense of order and control of a discipline continuously throws up more and more areas for investigation. But such questions are answered by other people on the whole, thus supporting the mode of 'synthetic-conventional' belief. Those who seek and find *new* answers, or answers which are new to their cultural community, need to develop other ways of seeing as well as the rational.

This stage bears a strong resemblance to Tillich's world-view B. As described previously, world-view A becomes inadequate for some people, as issues become more complex and as deeper questioning begins. Such inquiry is sometimes initiated by others, sometimes from within. Literalism wears thin at the edges. However, uncertainty cannot be sustained for long, and to begin with people's search for order and control tends to mean that the first reasonable answers are accepted, and more thorough-going questioning is suppressed. Tillich said that answers come from 'an acknowledged authority with sacred qualities like the Church or the Bible, to which one owes unconditional surrender'.[20] In other matters, people seek similar authorities, such as the scientists and naturalists who become media personalities. Whether or not the answers people receive are correct, the very act of receiving an authoritative answer helps many people, at least temporarily, to feel secure and more at ease within themselves. Nevertheless, Tillich maintains that world-view B, unlike world-view A, is rather more fragile. Questions tend to persist, and grow more intense; or the answers provided by authority may eventually cease to be satisfying. However, the outcome of this is not necessarily precipitation into the next stage of doubt and distrust of authorities (as Tillich's world-view model might suggest); it can be equally result in more questions, more answers, and even more shoring up of the citadel of faith. One of the problems with the 'synthetic-conventional' Stage is that communicating and absorbing the tradition of commandments and creeds (in addition to the stories that belong to earlier Stages) becomes an end in itself, and not an adjunct to other forms of belief, or a means to different ways of seeing.

Problems with conformity

The passion for order and the love of control lead to certain problems, which are particularly clear in some forms of religious faith, but which also apply to other forms of thinking and belief. While there is much in any discipline about which there can be healthy argument, and there are facts and figures which need to be checked and challenged, fundamental beliefs themselves are less accessible to argument or reason. Reason and conviction should not be confused. This does not prevent individuals and institutions from trying to enforce belief, using their power to persuade and to punish; and, given the need to belong, it is not surprising that some of those so pressured choose to conform. If they do not, they are often expelled and labelled 'heretic' by that or some similar name.

Beliefs can be treated like laws.[21] Religious practices and rituals can be treated like obsessions, and failure to comply with 'the way things are done' can lead to intense guilt and anxiety. Unquestioning obedience can be required by a church or a community, as in the worst kind of strict childhood. Symbols, while held as sacred, are so protected that attempts to demythologize them are fought off, as if in the very act of reinterpreting symbols the baby will be thrown out with the bath water.

Small wonder that Erikson suggests that the 'ritual excess' of the anal stage is legalism.[22] Faber similarly illustrates the dangers of conformist religion and thinking by reference to Freud's anal stage of development and to its equivalent in religious terms, where authority is one of the issues.[23] He isolates three particular examples of anal religion. The first is Phariseeism, where (according to the New Testament at least) an obsessional mentality insisted on 'dotting the i's and crossing the t's': where it appeared that man was made for the sabbath, and not the sabbath for man; where cleanliness laws were rigorously adhered to; where law was more important than liberty; and where 'you must' and 'you must not' seemed to be key injunctions.

The second form of anal religion is Puritanism, with its stress on status, on duty, on making money (without being seen to be spending it), on frugality and industry, and on achievement and good works. All these are ways of proving to oneself and to others that salvation has been achieved, and that one is a member of the predestined elect. A splendid literary example of such belief and practice is Mr Bulstrode in *Middlemarch*:

> Who could use money and position better than he meant to use them? Who could surpass him in self-abhorrence and exaltation of God's cause? . . . Profitable investments in trades where the power of the prince of this world showed its most active devices, became sanctified by a right application of profits in the hands of God's servant.[24]

In both Phariseeism and Puritanism, there is a sense in which religion appears not only to force religious believers into a straight-jacket of rules, but also to bring the Almighty under its control.

As his third example of anal religion, Faber includes

secularization. Unlike the first two, which emphasize
authority, secularization gives the wrong kind of weight to
autonomy. Faber points to the emphasis in society on
achievement, on status, on making money, on ownership,
and on the value of work, where the 'manager' has become a
central figure. While it is not easy to call secularization a
religion, it may be an idol; and it certainly embodies various
kinds of belief, including belief in the autonomy of man. (I
use the word 'man' deliberately, because, as the next chapter
suggests, women tend not to accord the same value to
independence, power or isolation from close relationships as
'man' does.) Secular values and the secular materialistic
sense of meaning have much in common with the Phariseeism
and Puritanism with which Faber associates secularization,
not least in the emphasis on doing and having, rather than
being.

The decline of religious belief has led to a new kind of
belief, which lays excessive stress on man's autonomy. The
increasing control of natural resources, and defence against
natural forces, has led to considerable weakening of the sense
of being a comparatively minor (if rather overrated) part of
the planet Earth, as well as being an infinitely tiny speck of
dust in the universe. While religion has itself sometimes been
an excuse for those in authority to play God, the decline of
religion has done nothing to lessen the desire for self-inflation
or the deification of humankind. Perhaps as a defence against
the anxiety of our own finiteness, we suffer the delusion (it is
not as constructive or as sane as an illusion) of self-sufficiency.
True autonomy does not obviate the necessity of belonging.

The legalistic emphasis is also seen in some of the historic
expressions of Hinduism, particularly in the worst excesses
of the caste-system. Zaehner observes that the untouchables
were seen as 'a source of pollution; their touch defiled, and
the infection had to be removed by purificatory rites'.[25] He
points out in the same context that, even when there was an
'onslaught' on the caste system, it was the lower castes and
the untouchables themselves who showed the most vigorous
opposition, because 'the caste discipline was far stricter
among the lower castes and the fear of being outcasted was
therefore the more intense'.

I am myself not happy with the way Faber isolates
Phariseeism and Puritanism, as if they were separate

religions, from Judaism, Islam and Christianity, which he places on a different, higher level. The three world religions include many other examples of groups with similar attitudes. Furthermore, it is easy to forget that Phariseeism, Puritanism and even secularization all arose from attempts to break away from the sterility of the established order. What commonly occurs with many types of new movement, whether they concern religious faith, political theory and action, or a new development in an intellectual discipline, is that they themselves are liable to turn into alternative or additional agents of oppressive conformity with the passage of time. Initially, they were attempts to find a new way. The risk is that any form of new thinking, within and outside the major religions, becomes yet another '-ism' or '-ology', with its own authoritarian structures and creed. One of the weaknesses of the linear model of faith development is that it does not sufficiently allow for this regressive phenomenon. Instead of another point on a straight road, Stage 4 might be seen better as a roundabout, which sometimes leads back to Stage 3, sometimes forwards on to Stage 5. Today's radical can become tomorrow's conservative. Similarly, radical communities may form about a new idea, or behind the leadership of a Stage 4 or Stage 5 thinker. But such break-away movements tend towards ossification and self-defence; they close themselves off against attack, fail to reflect upon their position and lose touch with what others are thinking and experiencing. In a relatively short space of time, their ideas become yet another of the ideologies, which Fowler believes to be the form that Stage 3 faith too often takes. There are numerous examples of this throughout the history of Christianity, but we also see it elsewhere: for example, in Buddhism. Watts comments on the Hinayana division of Buddhism that 'so convinced are they that this version contains the last word of the Buddha's wisdom that they refuse to recognize any ideas or precepts which it does not include . . . the Hinayana has become a formal and rigid, almost materialistic, school of thought'.[26]

The trend towards 'the heat-death' of any long-established group or community is not made any easier because of the way in which institutions (as they normally become) work. They function best when they are constituted of a large group of Stage 3 'conventional' members. Such groups tend to lose their most radical members. It can be difficult to remain in such a group when setting out in search of autonomy, and it may indeed be that those who look for their own meanings prefer isolation, for a while at least. In any case, at such a time, it is not easy to find a group of like-minded individuals. There are a few communities of faith, which Fowler would describe as Stage 4 or Stage 5 communities, where questioning is actively encouraged or welcomed, and is recognized as part of the normal development of thinking and functioning of faith. He suggests that Stage 5 communities (which I guess are very rare) have, like Stage 5 people, 'the capacity to understand and relate to Christians of each of the other stages' as well as 'the religious traditions of others as strangers'.[27]

One such community (although this does not necessarily apply to every member or local meeting) is the Society of Friends (the Quakers). Whereas in most Christian churches change is eventually forced upon a reluctant synod or conference by the pressure of outside events, I am impressed by the way in which, in each generation (every twenty years or so), the Society of Friends revises its interpretation of faith and practice, by a process of full consultation with all its members. The result is a breath of fresh air which is difficult to find behind the closed doors of much traditional religion. This freshness is seen by contrasting the style of the 1964 *Advices and Queries* with the 1988 provisional *Questions and Counsel*, for example in the clause on the care of children:

> Do those of you who are parents seek to share your deepest beliefs with your children, while leaving them free to develop as the Spirit of God may lead them? (1964)[28]

> Watch tenderly over the children who are in trust to you from God. As they develop in body, mind and spirit, their needs will change. They may be led along paths you had not anticipated. Think about the example you set your children, and be honest about your discoveries and your difficulties. Are you ready to share the happiness and problems of being parents? (1988)[29]

Even with such indications of responsiveness to the possibilities of change, the question remains how far such communities will allow questioning and rethinking to go?

The conservatism and sometimes repressive nature of faith communities is not confined to religious institutions. It is just as clear, for example, in the psychoanalytic community. The history of psychoanalytic societies includes a chronicle of sectarianism, witch-hunts, declarations of orthodoxy and heresy which is perhaps only equalled in the churches and in some other world faiths. Even political parties are not quite as hidebound, perhaps because they are almost completely dependent upon popular support.

In her history of psychoanalysis in France (and elsewhere), Roudinesco examines the difficulty which psychoanalysis has had in its organizational life. She describes the problem of combining a concern for the emergence of democracy, and respect for the ideas of individuals, with acknowledgement of the power of the unconscious. In attempting to organize in such a way as to give people freedom from powers outside themselves and freedom for the exercise of their own democratic power, there is a constant danger of 'liquidating the doctrine' that the organization is trying to defend. In the case of psychoanalysis, this doctrine is the power of the unconscious. If I understand the difficulty right, the paradox is that while the analyst tries to give freedom from power of the unconscious, the more danger there is that the power of the unconscious will be forgotten. (Likewise in the church, we might add, salvation is no guarantee against sin.)

For psychoanalysis, and in psychoanalytic thinking, the unconscious is all the more dangerous, not just because it is by definition unknowable, but because in enthusiasm for freeing people it is often forgotten how immense the difficulty is of genuinely freeing anyone from these unconscious forces. Roudinesco reminds us of Freud's discovery that 'men are subject to a destiny that eludes them and which therapy allows them only partially to uncover'.[30]

But she also comments on the danger that the more one is empassioned by a cause, the greater the risk of dogmatism and autocracy, and the less one encourages new expression and new experience. She states that:

> Against a guarantee for the ego, one then ends up with a cult of the master, or with the ardour of the mystic, which amounts to replacing the illusory freedom of individual speech with a religious adherence to the imaginary person

of a leader or a cause. To date no psychoanalytic society has managed to resolve that insoluble contradiction, but neither has any conceded that the contradiction is insoluble from the perspective of the discovery of the unconscious.[31]

Freud founded a psychoanalytic society, not an association for psychoanalysts, although that indeed was what it later became. The first psychoanalysts formed a group around a common cause, not around the protection of their own egos. Later, as they began to organize themselves, the defence of the cause was subsumed in the defence of a profession that sought to protect itself by making decisions as to who could and could not practise psychoanalysis. Thus, in the end, the concern for truth became a concern for order, for standards of practice and for the protection of the institution itself. It is interesting (as Roudinesco points out) that Freud accepted the position of founding father, but not that of political leader, even though he indirectly managed matters through his closest disciples.

Roudinesco's analysis of the institution that promotes but also protects psychoanalysis provides pointers to what happens in other professional societies and groups, formed to develop and safeguard other systems of belief. There is, however, a sense of hypocrisy in religious communities and in the psychoanalytic (and related) movements, in the way they act out and act upon their belief systems—a conflict between what they believe and what they do. In these cases, one might legitimately argue that 'they should know better'. What is it that leads those who declare the sanctity of love to be so cruel to many of their brothers and sisters? And what leads those who base their whole approach on the need to understand the unconscious—so blatantly to ignore the unconscious in their dealings with each other?

There is then a tendency for the 'synthetic-conventional' Stage of faith development, like the anal stage of personality development, to be one in which people become obsessed with issues of authority and order, and with the linked concomitants of sin, wrong thinking and guilt. Erich Fromm describes this obsession clearly in his distinction between authoritarian and humanistic religion; the former clearly emerges from fixation of development at this stage, the latter is more typical of more mature forms of belief.[32] Authoritarian religion emphasizes that humankind is controlled by a higher and external power, which is entitled to worship, obedience and reverence by very virtue of the fact that it has control. Fromm's concern about this type of theism or about some non-theistic political beliefs is that obedience is stressed above the two principles of love and justice. 'The prevailing mood of authoritarian religion is that of sorrow and of guilt.'

Humanistic religions, amongst which Fromm includes early Buddhism, the teachings of Isaiah and Jesus, and certain aspects of Judaism and Christianity, are distinguished by understanding 'God as a symbol of *man's own powers* which he tries to realize in his life, and not a symbol of force and domination, having *power over man* . . . God is the image of man's higher self, a symbol of what man potentially is or ought to become' (Fromm's italics). Consonant with the best examples of Stage 3 faith, and pointing forward to themes I introduce in the next chapter, Fromm also writes: 'Faith is certainty of conviction based on one's own experience of thought and feeling, not assent to propositions on credit of the proposer'.

Promoting autonomy

Although Fromm paints a picture of people as powerless when in the grip of authoritarian religion, he also observes that those who are the leaders and proponents of this type of religion actually exercise great power over their followers. While it is undoubtedly true that leaders may desire and abuse power, it is not as straightforward as it may appear to shed the power which groups give to those who lead them. I have already cited Zaehner's example above of the difficulties encountered in removing the caste system in India, as coming from those who suffered most from it. Because so many people are in this conventional stage, there are strong group pressures to keep the system stable, and for the group leader to be made to play a leading role in stopping the boat from being rocked. Whatever the stage of personal growth and faith development of the teacher or leader, there is a sense of being trapped into keeping their opinions under wraps, where they differ from the norm. I have met clergy who are afraid to share their thinking with lay people, lest they be decried for their views. I have also met many lay people who are afraid to share their doubts, lest they offend their clergy. Equally, in the counselling field in which I work, I have met new supervisors who are afraid to share their ignorance, and new counsellors working with them who are afraid to share their mistakes. In both settings, these are new and unfortunate twists on 'the blind leading the blind'. It would be much better for both parties if such collusive partnerships could be exposed sufficiently, so that each can share their false illusions about the other.

A more complete understanding of power must include the faith which followers place in their leaders, and the power with which they then invest them. Any power those who follow have, they proceed to give away by reinforcing the authority of those who lead them. While this does not excuse those who exercise power from using it to promote a greater sense of common responsibility, nor from sharing it where it can be shared, the process of doing so is a complex one. Education can replace ignorance, and rigid beliefs can be enlightened with more flexible use of knowledge. But educators and other leaders are often treated as oracles of wisdom, whether or not they feel themselves to be authoritative. Their words (as long as what they say is not too far removed from what people expect to hear) are swallowed unquestioningly. Some will resist deeper questioning, because of their fear of appearing to contradict authority, but others do so because they are afraid of the void that perhaps inevitably comes closer when they are given clear permission to ask the questions they are afraid to ask.

I observe later, as I have already mentioned, that the model I use in this book is essentially a fluid one; and I issue a caution against the ambition of forcing people to 'make progress'. My guess is that those who enter Fowler's Stage 4 thinking (at least as far as some aspects of their belief system go) easily feel impatient with those who demonstrate features of the faith development Stages 1 to 3. I am not sure, for example, that Stage 4 thinkers make the best teachers, since they are impatient with conformity and conventions, and want to hurry people through the basics to premature autonomy, and towards as yet unwanted freedom from submission to authority figures. Stage 5 patience is more useful, where encouragement might be given through

promoting the idea of movement and of the journey, without
commenting on the relative value of those places where people
may for the time being have come to rest.[33] What might
sometimes be challenged is the idea that anyone has ever
'arrived'. Those whose beliefs fall within Stages 3 and 4
sometimes share the 'know-it-all' quality that I ascribed to
our traveller's walking companions in the first chapter. What
might also be promoted is the relativity and changing
perspectives of knowledge; as well as acknowledgement that
much that we communicate is not hard fact but personal
opinion: 'perhaps', 'we cannot be sure' and 'I wonder if' are
all phrases that need to accompany much of the delivery of
expertise which is requested by many of those who are at this
Stage of development. Differences of view do not have to be
seen as conflictual—even if they indeed conflict. Doubt can
be affirmed as opening up new possibilities, as well as shaking
old familiarities. Crises of faith need supporting, but
collapsing faith does not itself need to be propped up. In the
context of religious faith, encouragement can be given to
identify 'I believe' statements, if necessary against what is
essentially the tradition of the church, now recognized as
such in the rephrasing of the opening words of the creed as
'We believe'. The Stage 3 need for conventionality and
conformity must not prevent fresh air from reaching those,
inside and outside congregations, who silently, and sometimes
rather guiltily, wait for permission to grow.

I have periodically related the changing patterns of belief to
the experience of existential anxiety. It is, for example, the
anxiety caused by questioning mythical and magical thinking
that leads to the search for definitive answers, which in turn
enables a reconciliation of sorts to be effected between the
original stories and information arising from other current
knowledge. Learning involves emotional responses as well as
mental processes; and emotional growth, in all its complexity,
is just as relevant as intellectual development in a changing
psychology of belief. The American, person-centred therapist,
Carl Rogers argues that learning which involves any change
to the self (and clearly questions of the meaning of life and
death impinge directly on the self) is often experienced as
threatening, and will be resisted, however reasonable the
arguments employed.[34] Emotional responses to new ideas
need to be supported and understood first, and anxiety

contained, whenever changes are suggested in attitudes and beliefs. Such shifts in psychological attitude may be a necessary precursor to changes in thinking. C. S. Lewis provides a good example of this in his Narnian children's story, where the lion Aslan (the symbol of Christ) talks about the dwarfs, who cannot see a glorious feast set out in front of them: 'Their prison is only in their minds, yet they are in that prison; and so afraid of being taken in that they cannot be taken out'.[35] Some people cannot accept what amounts to an almost water-tight argument, because it requires them to relinquish the even more water-tight security that comes from their fixed beliefs. Their minds cannot be opened, partly because to do so would threaten their whole self. This is as true of people who hold religious beliefs as it is of people who hold to alternative belief systems. The need for black and white answers prevents possibilities of more subtle ways of understanding. In the end this is a great loss, since subtlety and discrimination are important for exploring and understanding the complexities of the world, of belief and of the workings of the human mind.

In emphasizing the need for the development of the heart or of the emotional life, as well as of other kinds of knowledge (such as intuition), expressions of spiritual experience have much to inform us. In the Christian tradition, even the exact and ordered Paul is suspicious not only of knowledge, but also of omnipotent types of faith (such as that which can move mountains), and he acknowledges the centrality of the emotional response in the great hymn to love—'without love all this is nothing'.[36] To help people to develop emotionally—to be able to love—may be just as important as developing their knowledge and their faith. It may not be (as some like to think) that developing faith encourages better relationships, but the reverse process instead. Just as the reparations that take place in therapeutic relationship in counselling or psychotherapy can be mirrored in other relationships outside therapy, it is perhaps more satisfying relationships that are then reflected in fresh images of faith. Some of the importance of different aspects of relating is examined in the next chapter.

I am reminded of Winnicott's description of the task of parents as one of promoting personal growth in their offspring. He writes that children and adolescents will 'not be contented to find anything but the whole of themselves'.[37]

The phrase 'anything but the whole' is ambitious, but a worthwhile goal. But it is the ambitiousness of parenting, or the seeking of perfection, about which the anal stage of development has something to say. This also needs further examination, before turning in the last two chapters to other aspects of believing that go some way towards finding the whole.

Reaching onwards

Among the difficulties that are associated with this level of belief, such as the obsessional need to have everything in order, there is one which is especially relevant as this psychology of belief reaches onwards to describe (as far as it is possible) other levels of illusion. This is the need for *perfection* and for the *achievement* of perfection, which is recognized in psychodynamic thought as an anal stage characteristic; one which is particularly associated with hard labour, money, ambition and the kudos of success. Indeed, Erikson complained that his model of the Eight Ages was sometimes understood in this way, as setting out a ladder of achievement, and he warned against the 'success ideology which can so dangerously pervade our private and public daydreams'.[38] The difficulty with his Eight Ages may partly be the fault of the model, which is drawn as a series of steps; but it lies much more in the way his model (and others like it), have been understood in Western materialistic culture. I have already stressed that none of the models should be used as a type of league table to measure achievement, since modes of belief cannot be ordered in the same way as physical growth or social development.

The mystics make it quite clear that experiences of faith cannot be forced. Mascaró cites John of the Cross as identifying the signs of false ecstasy in a nun as 'too much desire to enjoy visions', 'too much self-assurance' and 'a desire to convince others that she has a great good'.[39] Or, to put it another way, a person may learn everything there is to know about musical notation, but without appreciation of music, such knowledge is nothing. Aesthetic appreciation may be enhanced by knowledge, but it cannot be taught or achieved by will alone.

To use models of psychological development, as a way of

plotting one's progress towards maturity, is itself an indication of too much concern with such matters—hardly a sign of maturity. The stages of faith development which I move on to examine in the next two chapters are open to such distortion. If they are identifiable stages (as I and others certainly suggest), readers may wonder whether they should have reached them (which I do not suggest). And if the readers have not, they may wonder whether they are in some way deficient. The developmental model can be used as a stick to beat oneself with, a sign of failing to reach supposed 'standards' of growth and maturity. Such a misuse of models is likely to feature strongly amongst obsessional people, who feel guilty when they do not achieve the high standards, set either by their faith, or (more accurately) set by themselves. Although some people certainly miss out by being unable to experience the levels of illusions that I shortly describe, many people have in fact some knowledge of them. They may not know them, however, through religious faith; or only peripherally so, such as through the tradition of art and literature which has been inspired by spiritual values. Indeed, it might be claimed that religion which has become too conventional, in the way in which this chapter has explored, prevents rather than promotes richer experiences of illusion, and that it sometimes has to be sought through other channels.

Even those whose faith models appear far removed from the success ideology of Stage 3, and the competitiveness of Stage 4, can fall into the trap of identifying a goal which cannot be achieved through intellectual effort, but is nonetheless variously called the 'highest level' or 'a peak experience', or even 'Stage 6' (which is numerically higher than any of the other Fowler Stages). Such phrases encourage the belief that these forms of experience are the best. I have been conscious of the dangers of such language throughout my study, and I may also have conveyed this mistaken impression through some of the phrases I have used. The illusion of progress is pervasive. Watts, for example, while not claiming that Zen Buddhism is the only way to Enlightenment, quotes the difference between Zen and other religions as 'all other paths wind slowly up the mountainside, but Zen, like a Roman road, thrusts all obstacles aside and moves in a direct line to God'.[40] Such a sentiment smacks of the success ideology which is also seen in the claims of other religions such as Christianity, where it is frequently said that other faiths may point the way to God, but that the supreme revelation is in Jesus Christ. Important though it is to discriminate between true and false ways of understanding, and between the positive and negative features of different belief systems, any hint of a hierarchy in a psychology of belief, or in stages of faith, illustrates the way the Stage 3 illusion has not been worked through sufficiently, and so becomes a contaminant of other types of illusion.

An obsessional need to achieve maturity has no place in a positive view of personal development, whether in terms of relationships to others or in respect of attitudes to faith. The reader may now understand my earlier caution about accepting models of human development as cut and dried. I fear that psychological descriptions lose their value if they are trapped in an overly rigid and ordered system. Although there is a radical break between Stages 3 and 4 in Fowler's model of faith development, the excesses of Stage 4 sometimes share in the same excesses of Stage 3, such as in wanting to subject everything to a single way of seeing. These illusions may be valuable for a while, providing temporary, and even necessary, self-confidence. But the most comprehensive and accurate picture of a psychology of belief allows for people to move in and out of, forwards to and back into, up and down, back to front, inside out and outside in: in other words, a truly dynamic psychology acknowledges that these different modes of faith and levels of belief are part of the whole, and present, if not always obviously and simultaneously, at least in rapid succession. Any other way of looking at belief is in danger of becoming too fixed to allow for the 'conjunctive' and 'universalizing' aspects of faith with which the final stages of a psychology of belief are concerned.

Notes

1. J. W. Fowler, *Stages of Faith: the Psychology of Human Development and the Quest for Meaning* (San Francisco: Harper and Row, 1981), chapters 15 and 16.
2. Fowler, *Stages of Faith*, p. 149.
3. Fowler, *Stages of Faith*, p. 127.
4. Fowler, *Stages of Faith*, p. 138.

5. Fowler, *Stages of Faith*, p. 128.
6. R. Goldman, *Readiness for Religion* (London: Routledge and Kegan Paul, 1965), p. 17.
7. W. E. Baldridge and J. J. Gleason, 'A Theological Framework for Pastoral Care', *Journal of Pastoral Care*, vol. 32:4 (1978), footnote on p. 237.
8. D. Cupitt, *Life Lines* (London: SCM Press, 1986), p. 34.
9. P. Lomas, *True and False Experience* (London: Allen Lane, 1973), p. 147. Lomas disagrees with Winnicott on this point, saying that training should encourage student initiative and acknowledge a student's knowledge of life experience from the very beginning. Nevertheless, Lomas's emphasis on student-centred learning does not mean that the training offered in his group is any the less rigorous, or values any the less the psychoanalytic tradition—with all its richness as well as its mistakes.
10. S. Freud, *Formulations on the Two Principles of Mental Functioning* (London: Penguin Freud Library), vol. 11.
11. K. Clark, *Civilisation: a Personal View* (London: BBC Publications, 1969), p. 66.
12. F. Capra, *The Tao of Physics*, 3rd edn (London: HarperCollins, 1992), p. 65.
13. C. P. Snow, *The Two Cultures and the Scientific Revolution* (Cambridge University Press, 1959). Rede Lecture.
14. Capra, p. 27.
15. Cupitt, chapters 3 and 4.
16. Fowler, *Stages of Faith*, pp. 151–73.
17. Fowler, *Stages of Faith*, p. 173.
18. Fowler, *Stages of Faith*, p. 161; J. W. Fowler, *Faith Development and Pastoral Care* (Philadelphia: Fortress Press 1987), p. 87. *See also* B. Reed, *The Dynamics of Religion* (London: Darton, Longman and Todd, 1978): the psychology of group dynamics adds considerably to the understanding of religious congregations.
19. Fowler, *Stages of Faith*, p. 165.
20. Quoted by Baldridge and Gleason, p. 234.
21. Cupitt, pp. 39–40.
22. D. Capps, *Life Cycle Theory and Pastoral Care* (London: Fortress Press, 1983), pp. 61–3.
23. H. Faber, *Psychology of Religion* (London: SCM Press, 1972).
24. G. Eliot, *Middlemarch* (London: Pan Books, 1973), p. 566.
25. R. C. Zaehner, *Hinduism* (Oxford University Press, 1962), p. 148.
26. A. Watts, *The Spirit of Zen* (London: HarperCollins, 1991), p. 22.
27. Fowler, *Faith Development and Pastoral Care*, p. 94.
28. The Society of Friends, *Advice and Queries*, 1964.
29. The Religious Society of Friends, *Questions and Counsel*, 1988.
30. E. Roudinesco, *Jacques Lacan and Co.* (London: Free Association Books, 1990), p. 224.
31. Roudinesco, p. 224.
32. The following paragraph and quotations are drawn from E. Fromm, *Psychoanalysis and Religion* (Yale University Press, 1967), pp. 32–51.

33. Fowler, *Faith Development and Pastoral Care*, pp. 116–17.
34. C. Rogers, *Freedom to Learn* (Ohio: Merrill, 1969), chapters 7 and 8.
35. C. S. Lewis, *The Last Battle* (London: Penguin Books, 1964), p. 135.
36. 1 Corinthians 13. 2.
37. D. W. Winnicott, *Playing and Reality* (London: Penguin Books, 1974), p. 168.
38. E. Erikson, *Childhood and Society* (London: Penguin Books, 1965), p. 265 (footnote).
39. J. Mascaró, *The Upanishads* (London: Penguin Books, 1965), p. 42.
40. Watts, p. 16.

FIVE

Co-operation and Competition

Breaking away

The fluid, dynamic nature of belief is not only a reflection of the unceasing movement of human growth and development — it is also a mirror of the inter-penetration of all life's stages in one person. Not only do we carry our past within us (our own personality, peopled by those who have made any impact upon us in times past), we also carry the seeds of the person we are to become: 'the Child is father of the Man'.[1] Above all, whether expressed as Tillich's existential anxiety,[2] or as Freud's hypothetical Death drive,[3] we also carry our own finiteness within us, even if repression conveniently lightens the weight of that prospect for much of the time.

At this point, and in some people (although what percentage it is impossible to assess), the dynamic element in belief fades, becoming stuck in conformity and conventions. Such a belief system seeks security against the trials of living and the inevitability of death; and the illusion of certainty coming from a static belief system (whether it be a spiritual faith or agnostic humanism) may collude with reluctance in facing the void. Since much of daily life for the majority of people on this planet consists of 'the ceaseless round, the trivial task', it may not be surprising that, for many of them, the moments when they have space to themselves are still filled with the conventional and the customary. It is as if the eyes dim, the taste buds dull and the wish for exploration of the new and the familiar disappears; with it, by and large, the magic fades. Such might be a description of those whose belief system (in all its aspects) stops with the end of the last chapter.

Others continue to grow — or more commonly perhaps find that staying in the same place, or with the same group, makes them restless and, like our traveller, they need to break away. In so doing, they place themselves once more in terms of their beliefs and values in the dynamic of life development itself, which consists of alternating periods of togetherness and of going it alone, from the first journey from the womb to the last journey into death. The timing may be flexible, but the pattern is an established one; most people move throughout their life between dependence, independence and interdependence. I return to more examples of this below.

This chapter reflects that pattern: first the need to break away, to find the self, in competition with established beliefs and groups; and secondly to find an identity of one's own, which is sufficient to resist the pressure of blind conformity. This chapter demonstrates the value in coming together with others in a similar position, where the richness of cooperativeness opens up endless possibilities. It is not only through others that fuller experience is found. In this chapter I also look at the importance of moving beyond conscious reasoning, to the discovery of new depths of meaning in the creative, the intuitive and the unconscious; and beyond human relationships alone to a deeper sense of belonging to 'Creation' as a whole.[4]

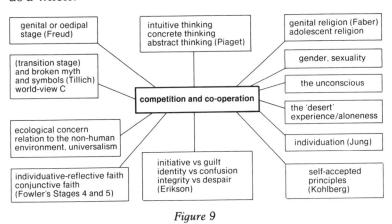

Figure 9

The elements of the central theme of competition and cooperation include the different aspects illustrated in Figure 9.

Dependence and independence

From the primal unity with her mother in the womb, and the other side of separation through birth, a baby is in a relationship which, if not as close as the womb, is close enough to be called, perhaps, a 'binity' — two in one. From the moment of birth, a baby begins to separate out psychologically from her mother, coming to learn that mother and self are different persons, implying that there is space between them, as well as intense closeness. It is only as a baby is able to separate that she is able to enter into a conscious and clear relationship. Buber observes that 'entering into relationship' requires a 'primal setting at a distance'.[5] Only then can we speak of a baby entering an 'I-Thou' relationship in Buber's sense. Winnicott, examining what it is that makes for the capacity to be alone as an adult, emphasizes the necessity of the basic experience 'of being alone, as an infant and small child, in the presence of mother'.[6] This early experience also forms the basis of the later ability to break away from the security of conventional belief systems, to engage upon the inevitably solitary task of finding an identity which is sufficient to be able to relate as a separate person with others.

If the crucial foundation for the right balance between dependence and independence is in infancy, the issue is one which remains and has to be worked through at different life stages. A toddler (even the word expresses it) tentatively moves away from her mother, a little further every time — although for a long while she still comes back to check that her mother is there. The separateness of the child of this age is also seen when, totally absorbed in toys and solitary games, she appears to need nothing more than the knowledge that mother is in the background. Another developmental step is taken when other children are seen as potential companions, and not just objects like any other — to be pushed around at will. By the age of four, a child is becoming a participating member of a social group: playing with other children, learning group rules, and separating sufficiently from home to learn from other adults as well.

Adolescent independence

The child's movement towards independence, which involves both the capacity to be alone and the ability to relate with others outside the family of origin, provides a useful way of illustrating a parallel in the development of beliefs and values. Similarly, the changes in relatedness that traditionally take

place during adolescence illustrate the stage of faith development with which the first part of this chapter is particularly
concerned, although (as with faith development) such changes
rarely occur at adolescence itself. Initially, the upheaval and
adjustment of major physical changes in a young person's
body give rise to a return to narcissistic pre-occupation,
which if apparently self-indulgent in a parent's eyes, actually
involves a teenager in as much agony and anxiety as pleasure.
The 'mix' of dependence, independence and interdependence
remains as evident in a young man or woman as in the child.
'The adolescent wants solitude and seclusion, while he finds
himself entangled in crushes and friendships. Never again
does the peer group have such a strong influence over him.'[7]
Erikson believes that it is in adolescence in particular that a
young person achieves a sense of identity and role, although
this is rather too narrowly defined an age for the process of
finding identity.[8] For most people, identity takes a variety of
forms (as a worker, as a partner, as a lover, as a parent, as a
thinker, and so on), which are achieved and re-achieved at
various stages of life. Many people seem to take at least until
their thirties before they begin to feel they have broken away
from the pressures and expectations of their family of origin
(often by then a more 'internalized' than an external pressure).
Small wonder then that identity in terms of belief is a lengthy
and sometimes ever-changing process, and that the type of
belief which occupies my concern in this chapter takes its
shape later in life, from the thirties onwards. Indeed, it is
often a crisis which precipitates the development of a clearer
identity for belief, when all the old answers provided by one's
belief system fail to satisfy or meet the present need. Such a
crisis marks the beginning of a journey of discovery for
oneself, a highly individualistic journey which resembles the
initial working out of personal identity during adolescence in
gender, role and work terms. Identity is no longer derived
simply (as it tends to be in Stage 3) from a sense of belonging
with peers or to an authoritative sub-culture, but from the
first signs of genuine self-knowledge.

There is a close parallel, as long as chronological age is
discounted, between the developmental task in the Erikson
model of achieving identity and role, and Stage 4 in Fowler's
model of faith development, 'individuative-reflective faith'.[9]
In each model, the stage is characterized by a breaking away

from assumed systems of values and belief. In both, the task serves the purpose of providing sufficient identity to engage in genuine relatedness, whether in Erikson's model in intimate relationships, or in Fowler's model in relating to other expressions of belief. While it is possible that values and meaning may not change dramatically, it is during this stage that those tenets which have been accepted tacitly now become more explicit, and ideas are thought through, no longer accepted simply because others say so.

The cost of disbelief

These important aspects of personal development are also significant parts of a psychology of belief. In my initial analogy of the traveller, I tried to convey how a child starts with a highly idiosyncratic way of perceiving reality; this starts with the fantastic, moves to the more formative myth and story, and then becomes firmly rooted in concrete and rational answers to the problems raised by perception and belief. Abstract thinking enables some new concepts to be adopted, but belief systems tend to stay at what becomes a conformist and conventional level. Those who belong to groups which exist for the promotion of specific beliefs (particularly religious and political groups) may find themselves sucked into a closed system of belief, where it is difficult to step too far out of line. There are groups, like some families, which maintain their own life at the cost of the development of individual members.

Even membership of a liberal and relatively free-thinking group may not be enough to satisfy the inquisitive mind in itself. It may be essential to move away from other people, however tolerant they are, simply because they are not able to provide the necessary stimulation, at least at such a point of development. It may be necessary to break free of former attachments in order that a faith that is more true to oneself can evolve. Winnicott's phrase for this is 'growing up out of' the religion of his childhood. Whether it is religious belief or other forms of illusion, such as a different intellectual discipline, there must be room to grow up out of the group and away from the parent community. What I am describing is perhaps the individual equivalent of community rituals used in rites of passage around adolescence in older, tribal societies. Indeed, the breaking away that I am thinking of may involve time 'in the wilderness', just as is often literally the case with ancient rites of passage, designed to teach the skills of adulthood, as well as mark the transition into it.

Religious thinking sometimes describes this as the 'desert experience', although, for those who have not experienced it, it can be romanticized as a stage of being alone wrestling with one's God. The desert experience can be much bleaker than that, without any God with whom to wrestle. As long as 'the Father' was with him Jesus could say 'I am not alone', even in the Garden of Gethsemane;[10] it was not until the cry of desolation at the time of crucifixion that true despair rang out: 'My God, my God, why hast thou forsaken me?'[11] For anyone who has been committed either to a religious faith, or indeed to any other system of belief which has sustained them, the point at which they lose their faith can be made all the more devastating because of the attitude of the group that they now have to leave, whether it is church, party, academic colleagues or friends. Those who are left tend to see such a move as retrograde, rather than as an advance into the darkness of new experience. The deepest loneliness comes when there is no God, no reassuring faith, no supportive group and little left of familiar props to sustain us. While such a negative response to 'faithlessness' is more common in religious groups than I perceive it elsewhere, I am aware that it also happens to others — in intellectual, political, professional and artistic communities — when they have to endure the same wilderness experience, because their challenge to conventional wisdom leads to desertion by their one-time colleagues and friends. I guess that such experiences are more common than we ever know, because we tend to drive such people away and hear no more of them.

Although I may appear to be describing extreme instances, there is a sense in which it is impossible for anyone to engage with issues at this level of belief without distress. There is inevitable pain, whether in allowing long-suppressed anxiety to the surface, which sends shock waves through the foundations of our belief; or in the more severe pain of dismantling all our cherished illusions. This stage is perhaps the epitome of disillusionment, far larger than has been known before. All that can be said by way of relief is that disillusionment without distress would appear to say little for the real value of the illusion that must now be given up.

Achieving identity

There are many stories of the wilderness, although none perhaps as apposite to this theme as the myth of Oedipus, doomed son of the rulers of Thebes, deserted by his true parents, and left in the wilderness to die. He survived, and was rescued and adopted by the rulers of Corinth. As an adolescent, torn by doubt about his origins, and frightened of the oracle's prophecy that he would kill his father and marry his mother, Oedipus impulsively left his home and wandered for a time alone, perhaps the safest state in which to be. Acting against his will, but as decreed by his fate, Oedipus tragically fulfilled the prophecies. Both through his own hand, and as a consequence of the initial murder, he was responsible for the death of both his natural parents. As a result he was once again forced into exile, although at the last accompanied by his daughters. The story underlines that only through extreme pain and distress, and in the wilderness experience at birth, in adolescence, and in the second half of his life, could Oedipus eventually achieve true insight.

The Oedipus myth provides the key to Freud's developmental model. Breaking away, the first theme of this chapter, has what Freudians call an *Oedipal* quality to it. Translated into ordinary terms, the phrase recognizes that children have to dissolve the intense relationship with their parents, through a process of breaking away: first at birth, and in other ways throughout childhood, but coming to a head in adolescence (when parents have to be 'killed off' in a metaphorical sense). Winnicott deliberately uses such evocative imagery when he writes: 'If the child is to become an adult then this move is achieved over the dead body of an adult . . . where there is the challenge of a growing boy or girl, there let an adult meet the challenge. And it will not necessarily be nice'.[12] It is also necessary, he said, for an adult to be able to survive this challenge, to be 'killed off' and yet, as in the death and resurrection myth, to rise again. Where parents go through this process with their growing children, after the stormy period of adolescent testing of boundaries, adult-to-adult relationships can be built, based upon mutual respect.

No child or adolescent can be made to go through the experience of pushing away, except involuntarily at birth. Parents cannot tell their growing children to 'be adolescent'; and if they do, or if they are too understanding of them, they ironically undermine the very act of rebellion which young men and women need if they are to experience such killing off of their parents. If parents are not hurt by their children, the Oedipal struggle becomes a game; not 'for real', as Winnicott insists it should be.

Similarly, it is impossible to make anyone question their beliefs and values. While in every sphere of human endeavour, whether religious belief or any other form of teaching, we could do much more to encourage individuality and originality, there is also a sense in which it is unwise to try to pre-empt the need for an 'adolescent' phase, either by being co-operative too early, or by denying a person the opportunity for their anger with established patterns of belief and thought, and with the institutions that represent them. The development of 'individuative-reflective faith' cannot be engineered, nor even built into an education programme, except perhaps in providing space for it, and being ready for it to occur, if and when it does. Winnicott suggests that adults need to allow adolescents to be immature, but without abdicating responsibility. They can provide, as it were, a 'frame' or a 'transitional space' (to which I return later in this chapter), in which 'growing up' can take place. Even then, the essence of a true desert or wilderness experience is that it does not come from our own or any one else's expectations. We are impelled into it almost like Oedipus by circumstances which are against our will; we find ourselves having to confront everything we had once thought was secure. There is no substitute and no soft option for such pain. Such a period provides few answers and no comfort initially. Only later does security return; and even when that happens, too long a period of security is perhaps a sign of the need to break away again. As one Sufi explained: 'I have stopped teaching because I find that I have a desire to teach. If this compulsion passes, I shall teach of my own free will'.[13]

Individuative-reflective faith

A genuine move into this phase of belief (or, as it is more often felt, 'disbelief') means interrupting reliance on external groups or authority-figures. Authority is relocated within the self, although other people may sometimes remain important to provide counsel and advice, and to share their own expectations. Fowler suggests that whether individuals can genuinely make such a move depends upon the character and quality of the alternative groups which they may join — in other words, that there is still some need for group identity.[14] I prefer to see this Stage as much more solitary, and value of the supportive group as coming later.

The move away from the previous relatively secure stage of conformity is typified by a number of tensions, which are (to use Faber's phrases): 'The dialectic between activity and passivity, between independence and dependence, and between defiance, and shame and doubt'.[15] Fowler describes similar tensions in Stage 4, between being an individual and being defined by group membership: as subjectivity and the power of strong but unexamined feelings on the one hand, and objectivity and critical reflection on the other; and as self-fulfilment, and yet service to and concern for others.

Faber's study is of the psychology of religion as well as faith, and he writes about an adolescent stage in the development of religion and society as a whole (note that neither he nor I are describing faith during the actual chronological age of adolescence).[16] Faber was writing in 1976, close to the radicalism of the late sixties, and he describes his own time as one of inner disorganization, of attempts at integration, of forming a life-plan, of finding identity and a place in the world, of searching for identification and identity, of experimenting with the 'primal themes of human existence', of the fading of the hierarchical structures, of more open rebellion against authoritarianism, and of the formation of new ideologies. The adolescent phase of religion, he writes, changes the concept of order, and moves more in the direction of the dispersion experience. (This reference to the dispersion of the Jews after the fall of Jerusalem in AD 70 is again to a wilderness experience.) In Faber's understanding, Jesus is far from being a symbol of traditional authority and power, but a revolutionary figure, similar to those in the counter-culture of youth that was more apparent in the 1960s and 1970s than in the 1980s and 1990s.[17] Like Bonhoeffer, Faber sees mankind as come of age, and the adolescent phase of religion seems to mark the final point of development. Unfortunately, as he stops short at this stage, Faber only makes passing references to what others would see as further developments, such as opening up to the experience of other faiths.

Faber's picture is an optimistic one, which reflects more the time at which he wrote than any permanent reality. It is another example of how much we live through illusion. It is not a picture which is instantly recognizable in contemporary European society. There may have been considerable breaking away from the churches, but often Christian values have been replaced by equally conventional secular value systems. (Indeed, Faber says as much when he uses secularization as an example of anal religion: see Chapter 3.) Fowler suggests that there is more to Stage 4 faith development, including the ability to shape one's own variant way of living—a bold step to take, because cutting loose means a serious move into the unknown.

I suggested in the last chapter, concurring with Fowler, that there are unlikely to be many established religious congregations in which 'individuative-reflective faith' can flourish, although no doubt smaller sub-groups exist where such questioning can be encouraged and shared. The climate for 'individuative-reflective faith' is often more bracing in the secular world, in universities, and in the serious treatment of questions of belief by the media. Even in such a milieu, we have to be careful about discriminating radical thought from the latest intellectual fashion—what *Private Eye* once parodied in its 'Pseuds Corner', those who espouse a position without appearing to think it through for themselves. As Fowler points out, the parallel in psychological terms is the adolescent who enters into an intimate relationship too soon in order to avoid the challenges of 'individuative transition'.[18]

Once conventional thinking and belief are confronted, an opportunity is made for a wide range of new options. We live at a time when there are many such new options for finding and asserting identity, often accompanied by a passionate and single-minded need for separateness. Such separateness gives rise to exactly the same kind of hostility (on both sides) that I have already observed is often true of adolescence. Angry separateness can be found in groups that promote consciousness for blacks, feminists, gay men and lesbians, as well as with those which radically question faith and order, and different moral positions. Some of these groups (often where they are similarly oppressed) can work together, but the fierce defence of their positions makes them suspicious of anyone outside who appears to want to compromise them. Perhaps the greater danger for radical groups comes when they turn from 'separatism that stems from a passionate defence of all they stand for', to the type of exclusivity that is more typical of established (and decaying) organizations. Today's radical becomes tomorrow's conservative all too easily.

A similarly diverse range of forms of theological thinking, which in collective terms bears some resemblance to individual Stage 4 faith development, can be seen in the options that emerge from Cupitt's 'Metro-map'. They branch out from, or are near to, what he calls 'The Crisis'.[19] By this he means 'the sudden loss of belief in an objective and personal God'. This is not confined to Christianity. Cupitt cites examples from Judaism, particularly following the Holocaust, and from Islam.[20] It is unnecessary to list Cupitt's examples of theological thinking that spring from the crisis of faith, but many of them emerged from the 'Oedipal/adolescent' over-throw of authoritarian forms of religion following the Reformation and the Enlightenment. Some of them suggest forms of religious consciousness that tie in with Tillich's world-view C, and with Fowler's Stage 5, 'conjunctive faith', which I describe later.

Important though this stage of belief is, I suspect that it tends towards reductionism and exclusivity; and if it progresses no further, it leads to narrowness of thought, and blinkered vision, sometimes even regressing to Stage 3. An important aspect of this stage of development is known as 'demythologizing'—recognizing myths as distinct from history, and looking for alternative ways of understanding them. This does not necessarily mean throwing symbols and myths out, but it can lead to reductionism—where the main interest is in what symbols and myths *mean*, and how they can be *translated* into more rational propositions and definitions. Myths at this stage can lose their poetic and evocative quality. The Creation story (to take an example I have used in other belief stages) now becomes a derivative of other ancient near eastern myths, and part of the Mesopotamian New Year festival. This may be true, and it may have its own fascination, but it also loses some of its magic when only understood in such a limited way. In Tillich's terms, symbols are 'broken', but they are perhaps not yet recognized as pointing beyond themselves. Analysis becomes more important than appreciation. Stage 4 indeed carries the risk (which Stage 3 people always thought it would!) of throwing the baby out with the bath water. A rather fine portrayal of this type of thinking, belief and moral behaviour in a group of Roman Catholic undergraduates from the 1950s can be found in David Lodge's novel *How Far Can You Go?*[21]

It is this questioning and yet reductive stage which inclines me in Chapter 2 (Figure 5) to place a question-mark between Tillich's world-view B and world-view C, as a more appropriate parallel to Fowler's Stage 4 than world-view C would be. The question mark indicates an interrogatory stage, prior to the proper use of broken myth and symbol. As defined by Baldridge and Gleason, Tillich's world-view C person has reached beyond the Fowler Stage 4 and into Stage 5.[22] Fowler states that the questioning Stage 4 person begins to have some sense of initiative over the symbol, although at first the translation of meanings of symbols into more abstract concepts sometimes leads to a sense of loss, grief or even guilt. For example, symbols and myths about eternal life may in the crisis of faith become impossible to go on sustaining intellectually. To let go of such myths and symbols is not just to experience guilt about overthrowing tradition. It is possible that it also arouses existential anxiety: that perhaps there is nothing more than this brief allotted span. Although some religious people like to speak of the great sacrifices they make in staying true to their faith, they may not realize that just as great a sacrifice often has to be made in giving up conventional faith. This is particularly so in a period of doubt where there is as yet nothing to replace the old certainties. Stage 5, which has its own anguish, at least provides evidence that myths and symbols, once broken, can take new life.

Small wonder then, as I have already indicated, that the new found beliefs (or disbeliefs) and confidence of this level of belief can lead to vigorous defence of one's own position, and little concern for, interest in or understanding of other people's belief systems. In the more fully developed position of Fowler's Stage 5, there is greater tolerance towards others, including those who adopt primitive or traditional positions. Those who have a Stage 4 belief system tend to be more critical and derogatory of those 'below' them, just as in every generation people tend to be more scornful and less tolerant of the generation or sub-generation immediately behind them in age or development. Stage 4 radical thinking is often accompanied by such impatience although, as in the formative years of late adolescence and early adulthood, impatience can also result in energetic concern for issues in society and for the rights of minorities. As such, this stage of belief reflects and incorporates Kohlberg's stages 4 and 5 of moral development.

Fowler observes that Stage 4 can also lead to excessive confidence in the conscious mind and in critical thought, and to a kind of secondary narcissism. Erikson describes the 'ritual excess' of this stage as elitism, which is a similar concept expressed in group terms. Some people may become fixed in this phase, not recognizing that life is more complex than Stage 4's emphasis on clear distinctions and abstract concepts. There may be some freedom in moral thinking, but not without persistent 'niggles' of guilt, as though in their liberation they had been more successful at overthrowing external authority, than in dealing adequately with internal authority-figures who continue to needle their conscience. This is why understanding the unconscious inner drives and objects is relevant for the next stage of development.

Transition

The form of belief that I have described above is at once freeing and limiting. It contains elements that might make for a more comprehensive expression of belief; although it also runs the risk of becoming sterile. I have already shown in the previous chapter how this can happen when the less brilliant follow in the steps of those who have broken new ground. The path gets trodden down, and becomes more comfortable for walking, but it leads nowhere new.

Stage 4, or the rational 'adolescent' type of belief, might be better called a transition stage, providing the first experience of a number of factors that appear with greater confidence in

Stage 5. It provides the first *real* and unanswered experience of doubt. This is both terrifying and liberating, and engenders confidence in letting go of the compelling need for reason and factual information. Stage 4 doubt is the first hesitant taste of what Keats described as 'negative capability', when 'a man is capable of being in uncertainties, mysteries, doubts, without any irritable reaching after fact and reason'.[23] Coleridge's phrase also supports the view that there must be space for the illusion which Stage 4 thinking too often wants to explain away: 'the willing suspension of disbelief for the moment, which constitutes poetic faith'.[24]

Similarly, this level may push a person into loneliness, and the isolation that comes with breaking away from the conventional group. Again, this sows the seed for a capacity to be alone, which Winnicott sees as 'one of the most important signs of maturity in emotional development';[25] while Storr posits a link between creative people and their constructive use of solitude.[26] These are again themes which I take up below.

The third aspect of this transitional stage of belief is that it is largely concerned with finding identity. Finding the self is an important step before a person can relate well to other people, or indeed to the non-human environment, as I come to later. What Erikson and Fowler describe at this point is conscious identity in the sense of a role, a sense of individuality, distinctiveness, and separateness from others. In Stage 5 of his model of faith development, Fowler lays greater stress on going deeper into one's identity, by engaging with the unconscious. These three strands—the ability to give up reliance on the rational and the reductive, the capacity to be alone with oneself, and the acknowledgement of the importance of the unconscious—form a golden thread that leads us further into the labyrinth of belief.

First steps into the unconscious

The 'unconscious' is not new to this psychology of belief. It has been there all the time, although this is not clear to the participants of earlier stages, only to observers. The unself-consciousness of children means the unconscious speaks freely but indirectly through magic and myth, story and symbol. It has little need to be *understood*, because it already finds expression. Furthermore, there is little room for acknowledgement of the unconscious in the ordered world of convention and conformity, although in its collective form (to use a Jungian metaphor) it no doubt can be seen at work in the dynamics of that sizeable group of people. Perhaps there are glimpses of the unconscious in Stage 4, although more by way of intellectual knowledge than actual experience. Reason and the conscious ego are still in charge.

It is when reason itself comes under question, and rationalization begins to be seen as yet another illusion, that a person may wish to find a more conscious place for the unconscious. In Fowler's Stage 5, 'conjunctive faith', people acknowledge that there are more aspects to their nature than they have hitherto recognized. Fowler sees coming to terms with the unconscious as part of a movement towards integration which runs as a theme through much of Stage 5. The task of integrating conscious and unconscious is a complex one, where self-deception is a constant risk. Identification of the fickleness of reason and the power of the unconscious (itself disinterested either in truth, lies, good or bad) was one of Freud's major insights. A second was the necessity of the presence and observation of another or others, normally an 'outsider' like a psychotherapist, who can act both as a screen for personal projections, and can also provide what might be a more objective (or at least a different) alternative to the limits of subjective experience.

In fact, the motive for seeking therapy is often an immediate crisis, rather than a dispassionate wish to explore oneself. Similarly, it is a personal crisis which often precipitates a person into the 'crisis of faith' of which Cupitt and Fowler write. The use of ongoing therapy to seek greater expression for the unconscious may develop from crisis work, and in this form more frequently occurs in people in the second half of life. Jung feels that this indicates the need to find some kind of religious meaning, although his definition of religion was a far from orthodox one. Finding 'meaning' (whether it is religious or not) might be closer to the real situation. Long-term therapy requires someone who is prepared to give up the illusion of independence in order to seek another's help, and this is more likely to be possible in the second half of life than in the confident self-sufficiency of young adulthood. It is

only with the experience of passing years that we recognize
that change is not as straightforward as we imagined when
younger, and that there is 'more to heaven and earth' than we
cared to admit in the rationalizing days of youth. The other
person, whose help we seek, need not be a therapist or
counsellor (although it is a sad comment upon the prepared-
ness of church ministers for this task that often this is so). It
may be a spiritual guide, a guru, a friend or a lover who
performs the same function.

Whether we follow the Freudian or the Jungian metaphors,
there is a wealth of meaning in the symbols people dream
about and imagine, and in the stories they hear, tell and
believe. In Jungian terms, symbols are expressions of the
universal archetypes of the *collective* unconscious, and to be
found as such in other religions and cultures as well as in our
own. Hence the value to which I later refer of journeying into
other traditions. In Freudian terms, symbols and fantasies
are part of the 'royal road' to the *personal* unconscious.
Whether we adopt the Freudian or the Jungian mythology,
the illusory quest is one of integration and wholeness, of
healing the split between conscious and unconscious: in the
Jungian myth it is the integration of extrovert and introvert,
anima and animus, thinking and feeling, intuitive and sensing,
the shadow and the self. In the more basic Freudian myth,
the ego 'serves three severe masters . . . the external world,
the super-ego and the id'[27] trying 'to reconcile their demands
with one another'.[28]

In the end, a Freudian definition of maturity is little
different from the Jungian concept of individuation; the latter
is defined by Samuels as 'the movement towards wholeness
by means of integration of conscious and unconscious parts
of the personality'.[29] Fowler has been criticized for failing to
pay enough attention to the unconscious, or to the distinction
between ego and self, in what appears like an emphasis upon
the functioning of the ego and of conscious expression of
belief.[30] Sketchy though his references are however, there is
no doubt that he intends the recognition and integration of
the unconscious to be one of the developmental tasks of this
Stage of faith, and that he points beyond the limits of the ego
to opening oneself up to the 'voices of one's "deeper self"'.[31]

Towards real ambivalence

The journey into the unconscious is as extensive in its potential as the journey outwards to other traditions and disciplines. In this context, I can only point out the possibilities and indicate the relevance of the widening, deepening vision of this age and stage. However, one feature of the integration of the unconscious requires further thought, if the tendency to split good and bad (present in different forms in earlier levels of belief) is to be faced. Integration, as described above, includes the Jungian 'shadow' and the Freudian 'id'. These two concepts are not identical, but they are equally open to repression. In Chapter 3, I suggested that there is a more thorough working through of ambivalence in Stage 5, and that the Hindu god Shiva is perhaps the supreme example of a symbol of ambivalence and integration. Christian teaching tends to perpetuate the dualism of good and evil, as well as of spirit and matter, although not all commentators accept such a split. A Jungian analyst, for example, writes:

> Jesus Christ has a Janus face. On the one hand, the Jesus face, gentle pastor of his sheep, wise moralist, golden sun of the noon-day world. On the other, the terrible Christ-face, numinous, indecipherable, eyes fixed irrevocably on the abyss of the timeless. No wonder the parson and his flock stick to the Jesus face. The Christ face, once seen, if only for a moment, would empty, as by magic, all those prosperous pews.[32]

If people are to start the process of drawing upon the traditions of other faiths and systems of belief (in Stage 5 terms), they need to be able to withdraw the projections that are commonly made upon anyone or anything that is different or strange. The stranger, or a foreign culture, forms a ready target for scapegoating—a process whereby the unwanted and unacceptable parts of ourselves are displaced outwards and on to another. Once located elsewhere, the unacceptable need no longer cause guilt or shame in us, although if such feelings continue to cause anxiety, the other (who is now seen as possessing the unacceptable) is also likely to be attacked. This was the function of the ritual scapegoat both in ancient Israel and in other cultic rites, but is just as prevalent in modern society (as for example in the Holocaust).

This process can be reversed however. When an individual or a community begins to accept the unacceptable as its own, there is less risk that the stranger will be made responsible. Projections can be withdrawn, and taken back to where they belong. The way is then open to stop labelling what is foreign in the stranger as 'bad'; indeed, it may then become possible to embrace the foreign in the stranger as potentially good and healthy. Instead of bad things being projected, good things might be introjected. In summary, as the tendency to split (which diminishes a person) is reversed, the integration of differences (which helps integration) becomes possible.

Some forms of religion may have had relative, if temporary, success in dealing with the problem of evil, but it has often been at the cost of someone else: either sacrifice of the scapegoat, or the diminution of the believer. Integration involves owning what was previously unacceptable, which is made easier when the nature of guilt can be altered. By and large, orthodox and conventional religion has not been very successful at dealing with sin, despite its heavy investment in the area. Although 'agin it', it has largely failed to understand it. At the same time, threatened Christianity has done a good line in 'the pot calling the kettle black', by accusing psychoanalysis of playing down the issue of guilt. Such attacks on psychoanalysis are fair game, but in this instance they are wrong. Clear distinctions have been made in psychoanalytic thinking between neurotic guilt and appropriate guilt; and between guilt as unhealthy self-punishment, and guilt as healthy concern for the other, leading to reparation.[33]

Kohlberg has shown how moral judgements in the early stages of development are made on the basis of fear, of bargaining, of pleasing others, and of conforming to society's expectations. In earlier stages of development, guilt or shame are often based more upon concern for what others might think of me, than upon any feeling I may have for them or for what they are going through as a result of my wrong actions. The need for forgiveness often takes the form of a desperate need for love, to be reassured rather than making genuine reparation to the person who has been hurt. In fact, psychodynamic thinking requires that we accept that everything that happens to us also involves our responsibility: we cannot blame the stranger. What we do wrong comes from within us and not from outside: we cannot blame the devil.

When we do wrong, it is a sign (although not a justification) that there is an important reason for it: we cannot blame ourselves. It is more constructive to try and understand ourselves, if we are to change unsatisfactory ways of thinking and behaving. A psychodynamic approach challenges defences (which religion sometimes erects) such as blaming others, and compels us to face the truth about ourselves.

The traditional wisdom of sages, sufis and masters breaks through conventional views on sin and guilt, in much the same way as psychoanalysis has done. For example, there is a clear parallel between the psychodynamic idea that there is no sin, fault or neurotic trait (call it what you will) in other people, that is not also somewhere (even if sometimes deep) within ourselves. Such teaching includes seeing the mote in the other's eye but not spotting the beam in your own, and other similar sayings in the Sermon on the Mount.[34]

Once more, these are complex issues, to which it is scarcely possible to do justice in a few paragraphs. Their relevance to a psychology of belief lies partly in helping form an attitude of acceptance both to oneself and others, in order to enlarge the horizons of faith. It also lies partly in developing the process of disillusionment on the one hand, and creating new illusions on the other; the richness of the symbolic world opens up immense possibilities for belief, such as in Coleridge's 'poetic faith'. Fowler provides a helpful illustration of the open attitude which is typical of a Stage 5 faith position. One of the women he interviewed was asked about her understanding of sin. She replied, 'Sin? I don't use the word sin, *ever* . . . I think more in terms of mistakes than I do of deliberate sin . . . In my own life I would perhaps describe it more as blundering because I didn't have the experience to handle things right'.[35] Later in the interview she spoke of sin as being cut off from God, but also she also preferred to use the term 'stupidity' rather than 'sin'. Her words are simple, but they express her ability to accept herself, to believe in herself and to learn from her experience.

Individuation and conjunctive faith

'Individuation' is a Jungian term, which I have already distinguished from Fowler's adjective 'individuative' (used in connection with his Stage 4). Jung's description of the psychological task of the second half of life as individuation actually links better with Fowler's Stage 5, which he calls 'conjunctive faith'.[36] As I have indicated, this stage is unusual before mid-life. It involves a more complex way of looking at faith, moving beyond the either/or of Stage 4 into seeing many sides of an issue simultaneously. It is a stage when people look for patterns and interrelationship, but not by forcing everything into their own mind-set, as tends to happen in Stage 4. Experience, including the experience of symbols, is allowed to make its own impact.

There is an air of certainty accompanying the breaking and the interpretation of the symbol in Stage 4, at least once the process has been established. Stage 5 is different, because the symbol is allowed to be itself and may therefore suggest new ways of seeing, including the possibility of fresh illusions. Stage 4 leads to a sense of order, which gives it some similarities to Stage 3, although anxiety and doubt are now allowed to stay long enough to challenge old illusions. Stage 5 exposes a person to the risk of uncertainty again. For a person to question something they have always held as true, as they do in Stage 4, requires courage. It may mean that some symbols can never be the same again. The Creation myth is 'explained'. But the Stage 5 person moves beyond this dilemma, into a frame of mind already referred to in Keats as 'capable of being in uncertainties, mysteries, doubts, without any irritable reaching after fact and reason'.[37] Tillich believes that world-view C people still feel anxious, because their uncertainty cannot be relieved by world-view A natural literalism, or by world-view B sacred authority—but they are more positive about the value of anxiety than world-view B people. Tillich associates courage with world-view C as well: 'Courage does not need the safety of unquestionable conviction. It includes the risk without which no creative life is possible'.[38] The broken symbol, related to world-view C, 'points beyond itself . . . participates in that to which it points . . . opens up levels of reality which otherwise are closed . . . and grows out of the individual or collective unconscious'. As Baldridge and Gleason add, 'Nothing but a myth or symbol is able to express the ultimate'.[39]

'Conjunctive faith' includes willingness to suspend reason, at least partially and temporarily. As I show later on, there is still need for other forms of illusion, including the 'illusion' of reality-testing. People can then enjoy symbols and fantasy, not as an escape, but as a way of learning and of bringing to the realities of daily life the riches of other fields of view. There are even greater gains potentially for the Stage 5 person than for the Stage 4 person, whose more limited interpretation leads to a more restricted experience of new dimensions. Rayner suggests that overcoming the denial of mortality can be a relief that enriches life.[40] I suspect the same is true of symbols; that in the end there is relief that a symbol does not have to be true in itself, and that there is relief in not having to keep up the pretence that it is. This process means reacquiring the child's (and acquiring the poet's) ability to suspend belief and disbelief. By its translation into new and even deeper dimensions, the symbol acquires even greater significance, especially when the symbol is allowed to speak for itself. In Stage 5 mode, when I hear the Creation story, it gives me one day, a sense of my unity with the natural world; another day, it reminds me of human responsibility for the planet; another, it speaks of the creative power of chaos; another, of the significance of naming; and yet another, awareness of the boundaries of time — there are now endless possibilities. Whereas Stage 4 implies rational control over symbols, Stage 5 once more lets the symbol take the lead, in an interplay between imagination and reason.

The idea of play is very important, and is closely linked with illusion. Play is psychologically necessary to help children construct and master different aspects of their world. Anna Freud traces a developmental line, in which the initial object of play is the body (for instance, a fist or a thumb), followed by a transitional object (say, cuddly toys).[41] Other toys are then gradually included, although there is not generally the same strong attachment to them as there is to transitional objects. They are more functional. Through playing with toys children learn how objects move, how they can be taken apart and how they can be built up into larger objects. Toys also serve as a means of exploring sexuality and gender, especially playing with dolls, as well as role-play games of doctors and nurses with other children. The capacity to play is used in education; children are encouraged to play with words and numbers and eventually with ideas. In creative and performing arts, children and adults learn to play with materials and with roles and feelings.

In a book called *The Play of the Imagination*, Pruyser argues that playing with illusion is necessary and desirable, and he places the process of making illusions at the centre of all we need in order 'to thrive'.[42] Like Winnicott, who wrote a book called *Playing and Reality,*[43] and Erikson who wrote one called *Toys and Reasons,*[44] Pruyser also celebrates play as a third world, 'a realm of mystical kinship with what is transcendent and universal'.[45] Drawing upon Winnicott's work, particularly on 'transitional space', Pruyser suggests that we live in three worlds, not the two that psychoanalysis normally describes as the external and the internal worlds. These two worlds provide only 'a truncated version of the options for growth and development'. The word 'illusion', he observes, derives from the root Latin verb *ludere*, to play, and Pruyser posits a 'sphere of the imaginative . . . located between and beyond the other two'.[46]

Like Anna Freud, Pruyser establishes the importance of a child's acts of discovery and, like Winnicott, he suggests that they are linked to transitional objects and children's play. Transitional objects, he maintains, also prefigure transcendent objects. These cultural expressions move beyond the hidden, inner world or the public, objective world. Illusions are charged with symbolic meaning, and lie at the heart of the visual arts, literature, the sciences, and religion and music; each of which he explores.

Like Winnicott, Pruyser takes issue with Freud, who explained the arts, science, education and religion as an attempt to sublimate the pleasure principle in search of the reality principle. I referred to the emphasis Freud put upon the reality principle in the last chapter. Education and science he saw as largely successful in finding intellectual pleasure in the exploration of reality. Religion he felt failed in the task of sublimating the pleasure-principle, since it simply renounced it. It was in art that Freud believed the two principles were best combined. An artist is able to turn away from reality and allow 'his erotic and ambitious wishes full play in the life of phantasy', coming back to reality by 'making use of his special gifts to mould his phantasies into truths of a new kind, which are valued . . . as precious reflections of reality'.[47] This is one of a number of hints that Freud gave of the value of fantasy and illusion, nearly all in connection with art and literature.

Freud tends to emphasize freeing humanity from what Pruyser calls 'archaic pleasure-oriented patterns into a sober acceptance of scarcity and limitation'.[48] By contrast, Pruyser argues that modes of play are not primarily sublimated instinctual impulses — they are rather expressions of 'joyous ego-relatedness to transitional objects, that is both adaptive and creative'.[49] A review of Pruyser's book praises him for making space for human transcendence and transformation within psychoanalytic thought: 'The sublime, and not simply sublimation, characterizes the genuinely human'.[50]

This sense of playing with symbols and the sphere of the imaginative is also relevant for formal religious belief and its expression in ritual and worship. I have already referred to the use of symbolism in worship in Chapter 3. Worship, like the arts or the natural world, has the potentiality to evoke and express feelings and ideas about physical, intellectual and transcendent experience, expanding the horizons of reality and leading us into our own dark corners of denial. Worship requires the ability to suspend reason 'for the moment' (Coleridge's phrase), and not to take apart every word, phrase or action which might be open to question in another context. This is more difficult where worship is highly cerebral. When reason is suspended in this way, ritual and worship may produce new insights, that might be expressed later in a different context, in more abstract terms. A parallel can be drawn with the theatre. The audience also has to suspend reason 'for the moment', to enter the illusion that is taking place on the stage and between the characters. They know (at another level, temporarily suspended) that the set is not a real place and that the actors are different people, but the audience allows itself to be taken beyond the drama into a deeper experience and understanding of the characters and, through them, to a deeper perception of themselves. Worship is also a corporate activity in which worshippers discover their own individual insights into the collective phantasies to which expression is given.

An imaginative illustration

Real life cannot fully illustrate the relationship between these levels of belief in the way that art can. Given the emphasis that I make upon the imaginative, that is perhaps how it should be. In Sara Maitland's novel *Three Times Table*, the author tells the story of three generations of women — a grandmother, mother and daughter. There is a fascinating, parallel process in the grandmother and the granddaughter. Rachel, the grandmother, is a palaeontologist, whose once important theory about the rise and decline of dinosaurs has been challenged by 'catastrophe theory': the dinosaurs perished in one cataclysmic world event. We meet her at the point when she can no longer hold her original views. What she realizes is that she has tended to interpret all the evidence to fit her particular theory, which is now fast becoming for her a 'myth'. As a scientist, she needs to move from Stage 3 thinking and believing — where her ideas have become almost as fossilized as her dinosaurs — to catch up with Stage 4 thinking, which questions established Darwinian theories and beliefs. Rachel resolves that she must publicly retract her long held ideas. She is like a world-view B person who can no longer fit her thinking into the original frame of reference.

Rachel lives in the same house as her fifteen-year-old granddaughter Maggie. Maggie rides the skies of London with a dragon called Fenna. Half-way through the book, at the point at which she resolves to retract her theory, we learn that 'Rachel's belief in her own theories was under assault from Maggie and Fenna'[51] — perhaps because Rachel now realizes, from her granddaughter's experience, just how powerful fantasy can be: if myth and magic look just like fact, what looks like fact may well be myth.

It is only at this point that the reader learns that Fenna first appeared when Maggie was five years old. The dragon, who earlier in the book *could* have been understood as a real dragon (even if a product of the *author's* imagination), is now partially revealed as a figment of *Maggie's* imagination, a make-believe friend. The author describes Fenna as 'the dark force of the imagination as well as its golden dancing; Fenna was chaos as well as order, and brought, on fiery, dragon breath, the full danger of the chasm'.[52]

The reader is held in suspense between imagination and reality. Rachel resolves to give up her dinosaurs, and Maggie resolves that she has to let Fenna go in order to grow up. In an exciting sequence later on, she rides the world with Fenna, before Fenna lets *her* go; and Maggie falls through the night sky and through the skylight of her house — or is it that she has been dreaming and is awoken by the skylight falling in because of some metal fatigue in the frame? The reader's imagination is allowed either possibility, or both: only the purely down-to-earth realist will want to look for a factual explanation!

The next morning, Maggie has her first menstrual flow. Growing up means leaving imaginary objects and people behind. The story illustrates perfectly the way in which Maggie changes from mythical thinking into realistic thinking, and from magical beliefs to the coldness and solitude of facts and ordered ideas. Maggie moves, as it were, from Stage 2 thinking and belief to Stage 3. Her grandmother, Rachel, has also realized that she must move from her fixed ordered ideas (as Stage 3 thinking easily becomes) to new ideas. She has to challenge her own 'tradition'. Her scientific thinking, moves from what has become her Stage 3 conscious literalism to Stage 4 realism. What is an appropriate Stage of thinking for Maggie is no longer appropriate for Rachel, although they are also both making exactly the same movement from a type of myth to a type of reality. Their myths are different: Maggie's is based on magic, Rachel's on scientific theory. Stage 3 thinking in Maggie's case helps her to let go of mythical thinking; but the way in which conscious literalism creates its own myth is also illustrated in Rachel's fixed ideas. Stage 3 belief and myth is all the more dangerous because it is disguised as, and apparently backed up by, 'reason' and 'fact'.

What makes *Three Times Table* even more relevant is that, as is appropriate to the theme of this mode of belief, it can be read on many levels at once. It is not just about three generations of women. It is also about different ways of thinking and believing. The reader does not know whether Fenna the dragon is real or imaginary. And it does not matter. In imaginative writing, the reader does not have to engage in a rational debate, as to whether the dragon really exists or not, or whether Maggie's fantasy needs to be explained in terms of developmental psychology. If the reader is tempted into Stage 4 thinking, the magic of the novel gets lost in trying to demythologize it. Such a book only works if a reader responds to the author's invitation to approach it on its many different levels of thought and belief. The reader needs to suspend both reason and belief, while not altogether ceasing to question magic and myth. This type of writing opens up the possibility of Stage 5 thinking and perception. It creates an illusion about the real world and real people, although it also creates illusions within the illusion, as it catches the reader up in the imagery and imagination of the characters, and in the space between them.

Perhaps this is most neatly expressed in the closing pages: Maggie has got rid of her dragon, and Rachel has faced her colleagues with her retraction; and the elderly Rachel stands on the steps of the museum where she works. She notices 'for the first time, that a medium-sized dragon was sitting in the upper branches of a particularly fine plane tree and munching a green leaf'.[53] Stage 5 thinking and believing opens us up to the same experiences and fantasies and thinking and believing that the growing child has lost!

'Conjunctive faith' is open to new experiences and to being taken by surprise. To be in this Stage does not mean losing touch with one's own version of reality, or one's own tradition; but it is to realize that 'reality' is also to be found elsewhere. Yet even the new meanings discovered in this way are recognized as being 'relative, partial and inevitably distorting apprehensions of transcendent reality'.[54]

Forms of relating: intimacy

Conjunctive faith involves relating in a new and open way to life experience. In essence, all belief is a way of relating (as might be expected of a type of illusion) because it serves the purpose of providing a transitional space in which the inner and the external world can relate. To complete this theme, I look at different forms of relating, each of which has its own set of illusions. I have already described one form earlier on: the relationship to the unconscious parts of the self. In the sections that follow, I examine: the relationship to one another; the relationship to the wider community and other traditions; and the relationship to the non-human environment — each of which is a separate aspect of Fowler's vision of 'conjunctive faith'.

I have dwelt at length in Chapter 3 and elsewhere on the relationship between child and parent. The Oedipal theme suggests that other types of pairings are relevant, and that illusion is attached to each of them. Intimate relationships make up much of people's concerns. What I stress here is the

ability to believe in and relate closely to another. I am not
thinking of marriage or sexual partnerships primarily. The
intimate couple *may* be a married one, but it may not; it may
be a close friendship, or an ongoing therapeutic relationship.
In every pair, each person needs to discover how to maintain
her or his own individuality and respect the other's, so that
separateness and intimacy co-exist. Rayner, for example,
describes intimacy, as 'being together but being separate'.[55]

Similarly, Winnicott makes a significant link between being
able to be alone and being intimate: 'After satisfactory
intercourse, each partner is alone and is contented to be
alone. Being able to enjoy being alone with another person
who is also alone is in itself an experience of health'. In the
same context, he writes about ego-relatedness as 'the
relationship between two people, one of whom at any rate is
alone; perhaps both are alone, yet the presence of each is
important to the other'.[56] He draws a helpful distinction
between liking and loving: loving, whether in a crude or
sublimated form, implies a need relationship: liking does not.

The search for bliss, and for perpetual intimacy of a unitary
kind, is one of those illusions which persists, and which
sometimes destroys relationships, because it is never really
fulfilled. Other illusions of relatedness need to supplement it.
Dunne illustrates the nature of one-to-one relationships in a
set of images which I cannot better, although over the years I
have woven his words into a fantasy of my own. He starts
by having us imagine the moment when Greek theatre moved
from a solitary actor and chorus to the introduction of a
second character.

Imagine, if you will [as Dunne would have you do] that you
are in an audience looking at a stage which is brightly lit, but
empty. Empty, that is, except for one actor, standing in the
middle of the stage, looking ahead of him into the audience.
He stands still, a solitary figure, in the silence, for what
seems like a very long time. Then from the side of the stage
there walks another actor, a woman, who approaches the
man, and stands by his side, turning like him to face the
audience. They stay there, side by side, each looking ahead of
them, seeming not to be aware of each other's presence. Time
passes. Then the woman turns to the man and says, 'We are
alone, you and I, and we cannot make one another unalone'.
He says nothing, as her words flow through him, finding

echoes in his own experience of what it is like to be alone on that empty stage. Then he turns to her. She has said all that needed saying, and there is nothing more that he needs to add. He simply responds in the only way he can, with a gesture, and he gently kisses the woman; then they turn back to face the audience, as the lights fade and the scene ends.[57]

We may be reminded here of Genesis and of God saying, as he looks at the solitary man on the stage of the world in the Garden of Eden, 'It is not good that man should be alone'. But what Dunne refers to here is a special kind of intimacy, a special kind of pairing, which may be present in a marriage, but is certainly just as present in other close relationships: between men, or between women, in marriage and outside of it—sometimes even in an affair.

Such a couple might be called 'soul mates', a term which religious people use technically, as well as a metaphor for any such close relationship. It is the sort of relationship in which people share their deepest beliefs—which are as intimate to them as their bodies; where two people speak openly and honestly to each other, and strip bare the pretence, removing the fig leaves of superficiality or the commonplace. There comes a moment in the development of belief when I may be able to share with another, hesitantly at first: 'I think I can't accept . . .'; or 'You know, I think I must be odd, but this is the way I see it . . .'. And the other answers, 'I'm glad you've said that. I have been thinking that, and wanting to say it, for a long time'. Such conversations go on more often than we think, especially in psychotherapy and counselling, although not so often in churches or in established groups, where only whispers are dared. Intimate speaking is reserved for people special to us, in special settings and special circumstances.

There are many spiritually committed people who speak of God as this close companion. Whether they mean this literally, as in early and middle levels of belief, or in a metaphorical sense, as would fit better with this level of belief, only they can say. 'What a friend I have in Jesus' frequently sounds like the former, although the tenderness and eroticism with which many mystics speak of their relationship with God would seem to indicate a level of belief which is far removed from the testimony that often sounds like a banal sentiment. Perhaps Dame Julian of Norwich or Teresa of Avila (to take two examples) were just better at saying it, but I suspect that in their spiritual experience there was a sublime quality that is absent in those who convert their relationship with God into a conventional car-sticker. As the next chapter suggests, it may also be that questions of literalism or metaphor are irrelevant for those we call mystics.

What might be read into images of God is the changing relationship; from punitive father or comforting mother to friend and lover. This is a major shift, not only into the poetry of love, but also into a more equal relationship. The Oedipal theme of this level of belief supports breaking away from parental images of God. The Oedipal tie to a parental image is replaced by a more adult relationship, based on companionship and support and not on fear, need or obligation. In some cases, God is lover too. That such a phrase does not raise the spectre of incest (since God is mother or father as well) is an indication that it describes metaphorical and not literal relationships. In theological terms, *eros* is integrated with *philia* and *agape*. These images are examined more closely in McFague's study of models of God, where her various metaphors, coming from a feminist theological perspective, seem to accord with Freud's understanding of mature relationships.[58]

Gender issues in a psychology of belief

The feminist perspective in both psychology and theology has seriously questioned the use of gender specific language, as well as gender stereotypes. Given the illusion that is inherent in all belief, it is vital to consider the issues that gender awareness raises in relation to a psychology of belief. Do men and women, for example, have similar belief experiences?

The question is made all the more pertinent following Gilligan's reappraisal of Kohlberg's study of moral development, and of other psychological models — nearly all of which have been created by men. Gilligan, who was one of Kohlberg's research colleagues, questioned his emphasis on justice as a measure of moral development.[59] She was particularly concerned that, as a result of his research, women were rarely placed in moral development stage 4, but mainly in stage 3. This made it appear that women were less developed in their moral thinking than men — which, indeed Freud had hinted at himself many years earlier. Gilligan went back to the research and discovered that women tended to approach the moral questions that had been used as a basis for the interviews in different ways to men. Women were less concerned with rules and more with relationships, with where actions might lead and with the history that lay behind the moral dilemmas. This sense of connectedness and responsibility seemed to be a feature in women, which Gilligan distinguished from the ethics of duty which predominated in men. There are many parallels for her findings in feminist psychoanalytic literature on the gender differences in the mother-baby relationship. Evidence suggests different attitudes in mothers towards baby sons and daughters, and that this early relationship influences the different attitudes seen in boys or girls, as well as men and women, both to themselves and to others.[60]

Gilligan's work seriously questions the readiness of psychologists and others to identify men and women, although the separate identification of a male and a female psychology also presents problems; one problem being the tendency to separatism, another stereotyping all men as 'men' or all women as 'women'. Freud believed that the terms used to describe differences in psychological characteristics in men and women served no useful purpose.[61] There might be an argument that cultural expectations and child-rearing assumptions have created differences which the integrative stance of this stage of belief should question.

Such is the position in a number of psychological approaches. The Jungian principle of individuation aims at helping people embrace the less developed sides of themselves: men accepting their anima or the 'feminine', and women their animus or the 'masculine'. In Taoism, the complementary nature of *yin* and *yang* is fundamental to Chinese thought: *yin*, the feminine, the intuitive and the complex; *yang* the masculine, the clear and the rational. There are also studies of gender suggesting that many of the stereotypes of masculine and feminine arise from the process of socialization, and need to be re-examined—to encourage men to become more sensitive to and connected to others and the world about them, and women to be more assertive of their rights of independence. Does this level of belief require the bringing together of the apparently 'masculine' and the apparently 'feminine'? Or perhaps it should go even further, rising above gender, like Paul's assertion that in Christ 'there is neither male nor female'?[62] Fowler sums up Gilligan's work as showing that:

> Moral maturity, for women and for men, means balancing responsibility and care with a keen sense of rights and justice, along with learning to deal with the inevitable tensions and ambiguities that this will involve. This may be an important dimension of the integration, in mature adulthood, of the masculine and the feminine modalities in our lives.[63]

On the other hand, these arguments are all put forward by men (and I am also a man). Men may have a vested interest in keeping women's identity indistinct, by suggesting an integration of the sexes and the ultimate blurring of their differences.[64] Freud in fact suggested that psychological development may take different paths when boys and girls are about four or five years old, although feminists have argued the divergence comes earlier. Golan identifies different issues for men and for women in the separate decades of adult life.[65]

There may therefore be significant differences in the content and style of belief systems in men and in women. When Kohlberg first wrote about 'stage 7' he only provided one example, that of Marcus Aurelius, and the importance to him of *justice* as part of natural law. As I indicated in Chapter 2, he took account of Gilligan's qualifications in his later work, including a further example of a Quaker woman, in whom *agape* was the main motivation for her 'stage 7' attitude. Faber also asks whether there is a different experience of God in men and women? The correlation between images of parents and the image of God, to which I referred in Chapter 3, is also found in research which Faber cites, where the influence of the mother image on the psychological attitude to God is more frequently and strongly felt by men and boys, and the father image by women and girls.[66] In another study, it was found that the idea of God in adolescent boys was more strongly marked by the concept of the 'Holy Virgin' than by Christ, although the opposite was true in girls.[67] Both these studies took place in a European, Catholic culture, and may have less significance in the more Protestant, British tradition.

These are areas which are open to much further study,

especially as women engage in the study of faith development. Questions of identity and separateness remain open, although a fuller expression of the distinctiveness of men and women might be for each to discover and acknowledge where the other is different, and to find completeness, not in all becoming the same, but in making the most of the complementary nature of those differences.

Forms of relating: the wider community

Just as in one-to-one relationships, there is the need to be separate as well as intimate. So, in membership of a group, the individuals who compose it need to retain and use their own identity while remaining fully participating members of the group. In large groups, distinctions have been made between membership individuals (who belong by conforming to group norms and expectations) and individual members (who retain their individuality while remaining full members within the group). Others simply retire from the group, either by physically staying away or by withdrawing into themselves. They preserve their individuality, but do not participate in the group.[68]

The 'group' has an unfortunate history. Large groups have sometimes become mobs or callous institutions, perpetrating some of the worst atrocities and persecutions in history. Even safe groups, such as those to which Stage 3 believers may belong, have at their best a way of diminishing the responsibility and initiative of their individual members. In the end, many Stage 4 questioners have been glad to get out of the groups that held them back. On a smaller scale, groups find less favour — with counsellors and therapists seeming to prefer 'one-to-one' consultations on the whole. Such a model has the same dangers and limitations as a parent-child relationship, where parent and child continue to cling to each other long after they should have let one another go.

In Stage 5 faith development, Fowler identifies a concern to meet with others and learn from them, giving up the isolation that is frequently a necessary part of Stage 4. It is important to test out one's thinking and beliefs, and to learn from the variety of ideas which a supportive group might encourage. By allowing others to impinge on them, Stage 5 thinkers and believers expose themselves to the necessary risk of uncertainty, and have a continuing incentive to review their ideas. Given their earlier experience of groups that have either destroyed or diminished, joining such groups may at first be risky and uncomfortable. In the end however, given a group which functions co-operatively, the experience is one which can be liberating and stimulating. The group is valued, as the analogy of the traveller tried to show, not because of the clear answers its members give to questions, nor for the security of holding common opinions, but because membership provides new perspectives.

For this to happen a different type of group is required; one where, as in Turquet's terms above, people are encouraged to be individual members rather than membership individuals. The most productive groups are not those that are made up of like-minded people, but of individuals with different life experiences and a variety of patterns of belief, who are ready to share their thinking, their feelings and their beliefs, without forcing their own experience upon others. Members are prepared to respond to opinions not with cutting criticism, but with their own ideas. They recognize that the differences allow each person to gain from the other. Such groups seldom end their meeting with agreements, resolutions or conclusions, but members may leave feeling they have expressed themselves and have learned from others.

Part of this wider dimension of sharing with others also involves the discovery of ideas, images and stories from other world faiths. This Stage of faith development recognizes the relativity of religious traditions, not so much in terms of how they compare and relate to each other (in a quasi-competitive way); but in recognizing that they are all illusions, attempting to mediate and interpret what each sees as ultimate 'reality'. People in Stage 4 accept that others think differently, but sometimes place excessive confidence in their own system of thought and belief. In Stage 5, complementarity replaces competition, as people learn that other ways of understanding can inform their own. Dunne adopts the phrase 'passing over' to illustrate how new perspectives appear from passing over to other faiths, and immersing oneself in them, before making the journey back to one's own faith tradition, newly enriched by the experience of the other.[69] He does not mean syncretism, whereby features of other faiths are incorporated into one's own. Although this may happen, or parallels may be found, what Dunne proposes is that such a journey makes a person look across differently at their own belief system, even if they adopt little or nothing of what they have seen 'on the other side'.

A telling illustration of Dunne's 'passing over' is found in a folk tale, which takes various forms in different countries — which fact alone shows the convergence of key motifs in various cultural traditions. In England, I believe the story is known as the Tailor of Norwich. In the Hassidic tradition of Eastern Europe, it is the story of Rabbi Isaac of Cracow, who dreamed several nights running that if he was to dig beneath the King Charles bridge leading to the royal palace in Prague he would find buried treasure. The persistence of this dream impelled him to walk to Prague — a long way for an old man — and when he got there, he found the scene just as he had dreamed it, with the bridge under which he would need to dig. Unfortunately, the bridge was patrolled day and night by the royal guard, whose officer eventually noticed Rabbi Isaac loitering — waiting in vain for the moment when the sentries went off duty. The officer asked the Rabbi what he was doing.

Innocently, Rabbi Isaac told the captain of the guard about his dream, that if he were to dig under the bridge leading to the royal palace in Prague, he would find buried treasure. The officer roared with laughter, and slapped the Rabbi on the back. 'Dreams', he mocked, 'Dreams? You believe in dreams? What nonsense! Why, I had a dream like that too: I dreamed that if I went to Cracow, and to such and such a street, in such and such a house I would find a stove; and if I dug under the stove I would find buried treasure. But me, I don't believe in dreams!'

'Thank you, Sir', said the Rabbi, feigning a salute and scuttling quickly away to begin the long trek home. For he had recognized the street and the house as his own; and when he got home, he dug under the stove, and found the buried treasure. But he had to make the journey, and listen to another's dream, before he found the treasure he had dreamed of, buried all the time in his own back room.

Recognition and acknowledgement of the equal value of other faiths varies greatly in the world religions. Christianity and Islam have a reputation for exclusivity, as well as for the persecution or conversion of those who espouse other faiths. Dunne's 'passing over' might be most appropriate to those traditions, where the illusion of the supremacy of their own creed makes genuine dialogue difficult. Within Hinduism and Buddhism there is greater acceptance that different paths lead to an identical truth, although perhaps little real interest in other faiths. Zaehner describes a liberal Hindu as having little use for religious syncretism, but 'that it is his dearest wish that each religious tradition should develop and grow in accordance with its own native genius, while honouring and respecting the other great religions as being paths converging upon the same central point'.[70] Nevertheless, the politics of India and Sri Lanka (to take just two examples) make it clear that some Hindu and Buddhist groups, as much as some Christian or Muslim sects, can be religious militants and bigots.

Atheism and some forms of humanism can sometimes be expressed with similar militancy and bigotry, although a critical but tolerant attitude is more usual in those who have thought out their position. In effect, the stages of belief are just as evident in different expressions of agnosticism and atheism as they are in any religious faith. In earlier stages of atheistic or agnostic belief, religious faith is usually seen as completely alien or misguided; but in this later stage there are clear examples of the acknowledgement of the richness of religious traditions. Deeper appreciation of religious symbolism is not prevented by intellectual scepticism. The television and theatre producer and twentieth-century *savant* Jonathan Miller is quoted as saying of himself:

> Never underestimate the piety of atheists. Those of us who have no religious belief, who find ourselves thrown into the unsupervised affair of an empty cosmos with no captain on the bridge might still agree it would, as Hemingway said, be pretty to think otherwise. And that's more than saying the Incarnation is a nice idea. It's one of the greatest ideas, on a par with the invention of the wheel. It got things going. It extended the scope of human capabilities and our understanding of what it's like to be us. You'd have to be an insensible clod not to be moved by the Incarnation at something beyond the level of a story.[71]

Tolerance, or more positive acceptance of the values of other beliefs is a mark of this developmental stage. The risk is that tolerance leads to a *laissez-faire* attitude that ceases to be concerned about differences, becomes pessimistic about the possibility of change and turns a blind eye to injustice. Fowler identifies this as one of the dangers of this Stage: that it can lead to paralysing passivity and inaction, and to complacency or cynical withdrawal, as if accepting the paradoxical nature of truth means that there is little point in doing anything. Because there is a basic division in the experience of this Stage—between a vision of a transformed world, but recognizing a world that is untransformed—the temptation is to think that nothing can be done about it. If there is any loss from moving from Stage 4 into Stage 5, sometimes it can be that concern for others is not always translated so enthusiastically into action.

There also needs to be space in any system of belief for intolerance, particularly towards other belief systems that threaten the rights of others. In a polemical pamphlet, A. N. Wilson examines the right to 'live and let live'.[72] He does not wish it to make it illegal to believe nonsense, but he is concerned that 'large organizations of people who believe what others think is nonsense' are accorded such great power. He names the Pope, the Ayatollah Khamenei and others as representatives of that type of formal, organized religion, which believes it has special rights and privileges, and has the power to frighten and to threaten others who do not agree. His pamphlet is an assertive and angry piece, written by someone who is clearly disillusioned with religious liberalism. But it is an important corrective to accepting as legitimate opinion everything which those of different faiths have to say. It is also a pointer towards the intolerance of some of the most renowned and respected spiritual leaders of world faiths in the face of injustice and infringement of the rights of others. This aspect of belief, which involves turning a universal vision into practical action, is one which I examine further in the next chapter.

Forms of relating: the non-human environment

Artists, poets, scientists, mystics and theologians are all concerned with the natural environment, in one way or another. They 'believe' in it, and they draw upon it for much of their creativity. But psychologists and psychotherapists have been extraordinarily deficient generally in the attention they have paid to the part non-human factors play in personal development and functioning. Given the intense relationship which artists and scientists have with the natural world (whether portraying, or analysing it), it must also form a significant part of a psychology of belief.

Freud is one of a few psychoanalysts who comment on humans' relationship with nature. His use of anthropological studies helps him to recognize the relevance of the bond. He observes that many rational people place a gulf between their own nature and that of animals, for example denying the latter a soul. He notes that this 'piece of arrogance is still as foreign to the child as it is to the savage or to primitive man . . . the result of a later, more pretentious stage of development'. Freud's hope that Darwinism had put an end to this human presumptuousness has sadly not been borne out in a century which has seen the virtual rape of the environment.[73] He points to myths where gods take animal shape, and to examples of children's stories of animals that talk and think. We have to return to ancient, 'tribal' beliefs and societies to find clear evidence of human affinity with the Earth and with fellow species in their myths, stories, and customs.

The natural world and ordinary objects have the capacity to provide a stability which the promises held out in human relationships cannot always fulfil. Searles quotes another as writing: 'One of my earliest recollections is that chairs and tables *always kept the same look*, in a way that people did not, and that I was awed by the sameness of that appearance'.[74] Klein quotes one of her patients who 'from earliest childhood . . . found comfort and satisfaction in being out of doors'. Klein somewhat reductively interpreted his joy in one session when he described a journey into the hills, as being nature representing beauty and goodness, 'the only good object he had taken into himself'. Her patient's reply was that this was only partially true, because nature also contained a lot of aggression, and that he was not wholly good in his relation to the countryside—as a boy he would rob nests. As he put it, in loving nature he had 'taken in an integrated object'.[75]

Such a deep sense of identity with nature is too readily interpreted by analysts and pragmatists as an escape, a flight or a defence against the disillusionment in key human relationships. I doubt myself whether the ability to relate fully and in equal manner to oneself, to a partner in intimacy, to groups and to the natural world is any more than an ideal picture of a balanced life. People vary in the particular relationships which they find most natural to them and most fulfilling. Some forms of belief have demonstrated a deep response to and respect for the natural world, including forms of pantheism and animism, and some aspects of eastern religion. They support an integrated view, as in Hindu thought where the human soul 'participates in, is of the same nature as, or is actually identical with the immortal Brahman which sustains and ensouls the entire objective cosmos'.[76] Other faiths have split the material world from the spiritual and, as I have indicated earlier, have had little regard for either the welfare of the material on the one hand, or care for the spiritual on the other. The western secular belief in the supremacy of humanity and of reason, for example, risks losing touch with the environment. Yet the universalizing vision which the final chapter examines is empty unless the universe is included in it; or, more accurately, unless the believer sets herself or himself in context in the infinite vastness of the non-human environment.

Integration

This chapter has been largely concerned with the widening experience that extends the content and resources of belief. Disillusionment with Stage 3 conventionality leads to Stage 4 rationality, while disillusion with Stage 4 reductionism leads to the 'coming together' of different aspects in Stage 5 'conjunctive faith'. An alternative term might be 'integrative' faith, although it is not one which Fowler chooses. It expresses what Erikson also conveys in his use of the term 'ego integrity' as the central issue of old age. An ageing person, looking back over her or his life, often seeks an integration of experience, reclaiming and reworking their past, before they are able to let it go. Believing in themselves, and in the balance of good experience over bad, they are enabled to forgive and overcome aspects of their life that have gone wrong or where mistakes might have been made. Where this process is successful, it contributes to ego integrity. Failure to achieve the task may lead to despair and disillusionment in its most negative sense.

Similarly, this higher level of belief involves a type of integration which is able to draw on a life's experience of varieties of belief. Stage 5 is not an end in itself. It is just one more level, which needs to be included with the other forms of illusion that the previous two chapters have described. Reality thinking and rationality, for example, remain as important as ever, just as myth and magic must never be lost. Illusion needs to be framed and boundaried, so that it does not spin off into chaos or the void. The artist must paint within a frame, the sculptor carve within the limits of the stone, and the poet must write within the realities of metre and form. Dylan Thomas writes of 'my craft and sullen art', implying both technical as well as the creative aspects to his work.[77] Similarly, the physicist Capra describes how Newtonian physics and classical mechanics have been eroded by twentieth-century physics, although 'this does not mean that Newton's model is "wrong", or that quantum theory and relativity theory are "right". All these models are approximations which are valid for a certain range of phenomena'.[78] The novelist Nicholas Mosley expresses this similarity in relation to mathematics in the notes of a philosophy lecturer: 'Reality is not a metaphor we construct from mathematics: mathematics is one of our metaphors for reality'; also (anticipating my observations in the next chapter), 'if we try to put knowledge of this kind into words, are we not back in the trap of language'.[79] Only as we move beyond this range are new models needed to replace old ones, but each model remains valid within certain limits. Each scientific world-view still has its uses.[80] From within the Sufi tradition there is confirmation of the viability of different kinds of knowledge: intellectualism, emotionalism, and 'real knowledge, which is called the Knowledge of Reality beyond the boundaries of thought and sense'.[81] Such is the knowledge to which Sufis attain but, as the Sufi passage shows, they continue to validate the other forms as well.

Despite such examples of comprehensiveness, and the tolerance and integration found in the form of belief described in this chapter, there remains a tendency to isolate and elevate one form of knowledge, one sort of experience or one type of approach to understanding above all others, and to lose sight of the conventional and the mundane. This is especially true of the spiritual tradition which the next chapter addresses, where the attempt is made to move beyond the limitations of images, words and other illusions to the 'ultimate'. The next chapter includes the near impossible task of putting into words states of mind which those who have known them say are beyond description. I am conscious that, limited though they are, mundane and conventional words are all I have. To use an analogy, words are like the images and symbols of the early levels of belief, and structure and sentences are like the middle level of belief; both words and structure are necessary in order to describe and make sense of higher levels of belief. Insofar as they work, the reader may agree that, if the whole is to be described and perceived, none of the constituent elements in this psychology of belief can ever be left behind, however far a person may reach. All are part of the whole.

Notes

1. W. Wordsworth, 'My Heart Leaps Up'.
2. P. Tillich, *The Courage to Be* (New York: Nisbet, 1952).
3. S. Freud, *Beyond the Pleasure Principle* (London: Penguin Freud Library), vol. 11.
4. I use 'Creation' as another metaphor, which does not necessarily imply a 'Creator'.
5. M. Buber, 'Distance and relation', *Psychiatry*, 20 (1957), pp. 97–104.
6. D. W. Winnicott, 'The capacity to be alone' in D. W. Winnicott, *The Maturational Processes and the Facilitating Environment* (London: Hogarth Press, 1965), p. 30.
7. G. Stanley Hall, writing in 1916, and quoted in R. Muuss, *Theories of Adolescence*, 2nd edn (New York: Random House, 1968).
8. E. Erikson, *Identity, Youth and Crisis* (London: Faber & Faber, 1968).
9. J. W. Fowler, *Stages of Faith: the Psychology of Human Development and the Quest for Meaning* (San Francisco: Harper and Row, 1981), pp. 174–83.
10. John 16. 32.
11. Mark 15. 34.
12. D. W. Winnicott, *Playing and Reality* (London: Penguin Books, 1974), pp. 170 and 176.
13. I. Shah, *The Way of the Sufi* (London: Penguin Books, 1974), p. 196.
14. Fowler, *Stages of Faith*, pp. 178–9.
15. H. Faber, *Psychology of Religion* (London: SCM Press, 1976), p. 195. The phrases are in fact lifted from an earlier stage.

16. Faber, pp. 285–318.
17. Faber, p. 313.
18. Fowler, *Stages of Faith*, p. 178.
19. D. Cupitt, *Life Lines* (London: SCM Press, 1986), chapter 9.
20. Cupitt, pp. 107–8.
21. D. Lodge, *How Far Can You Go?* (London: Secker & Warburg, 1980).
22. W. E. Baldridge and J. J. Gleason, 'A Theological Framework for Pastoral Care', *Journal of Pastoral Care*, 32:4 (1978), p. 235.
23. F. Page (ed.), *The Letters of John Keats* (Oxford University Press, 1954), p. 86.
24. S. T. Coleridge, *Biographia Literaria*, ed. J. Engell and W. J. Bate (London: Routledge and Kegan Paul, 1983), collected works, vol. 7:2, chapter 14, p. 6.
25. Winnicott, *The Maturational Processes and the Facilitating Environment*, p. 29.
26. A. Storr, *Solitude* (London: Flamingo, 1989).
27. S. Freud, *New Introductory Lectures on Psychoanalysis* (London: Penguin Freud Library), vol. 2, pp. 110–11.
28. S. Freud, *An Outline of Psychoanalysis* (London: Penguin Freud Library), vol. 15, pp. 377–8.
29. A. Samuels, *Jung and the Post-Jungians* (London: Routledge and Kegan Paul, 1985), p. 101.
30. M. Ford-Grabowsky, 'The Fullness of the Christian Faith Experience: Dimensions Missing in Faith Development Theory', *Journal of Pastoral Care*, 61:1 (1987).
31. Fowler, *Stages of Faith*, p. 198.
32. A. McGlashan, *Savage and Beautiful Country* (London: Chatto & Windus, 1966).
33. M. Klein, 'On the Theory of Anxiety and Guilt', in M. Klein, *Envy and Gratitude and Other Works 1946–1963* (London: Hogarth Press, 1975).
34. Matthew 7. 1–5.
35. Fowler, *Stages of Faith*, p. 196.
36. Fowler, *Stages of Faith*, pp. 183–98.
37. Page, p. 86. See footnote 23.
38. P. Tillich, *Dynamics of Faith* (New York: Harper, 1957), p. 101.
39. Baldridge and Gleason, p. 235; and quoting Tillich, *Dynamics of Faith*, pp. 41–3.
40. E. Rayner, *Human Development*, 2nd edn (London: Allen and Unwin, 1978), p. 171.
41. A. Freud, *Normality and Pathology in Childhood* (London: Penguin Books, 1973), pp. 64–76.
42. P. W. Pruyser, *The Play of the Imagination: Toward a Psychoanalysis of Culture* (New York: International Universities Press, 1983), p. 210.
43. Winnicott, *Playing and Reality*.
44. E. Erikson, *Toys and Reasons* (London: Marion Boyars, 1978).
45. Pruyser, p. 200.
46. Pruyser, p. 165.
47. S. Freud, *Formulations on the Two Principles of Mental Functioning* (London: Penguin Freud Library), vol. 11, pp. 41–2.

48. Pruyser, p. 204.
49. Pruyser, pp. 205–6.
50. J. B. Ashbrook, 'Review of "The Play of the Imagination: Toward a Psychoanalysis of Culture"', *Journal of Pastoral Care*, 39:2 (1985), p. 195.
51. S. Maitland, *Three Times Table* (London: Virago Press, 1990), p. 109.
52. Maitland, p. 109.
53. Maitland, p. 215.
54. Fowler, *Stages of Faith*, p. 198.
55. Rayner, p. 34.
56. Winnicott, *The Maturational Processes and the Facilitating Environment*, p. 31.
57. J. S. Dunne, *Time and Myth* (London: SCM Press, 1973), pp. 106–7.
58. S. McFague, *Models of God* (London: Fortress Press and SCM Press, 1987).
59. C. Gilligan, *In a Different Voice: Psychological Theory and Women's Development* (Harvard University Press, 1982).
60. E. Belotti, *Little Girls* (London: Readers and Writers Co-operative, 1985); N. Chodorow, *The Reproduction of Mothering* (London: University of California Press, 1978); D. Dinnerstein, *The Rocking of the Cradle and the Ruling of the World* (London: The Women's Press, 1987).
61. S. Freud, *New Introductory Lectures on Psychoanalysis*, pp. 147–9.
62. Galatians 3. 28.
63. J. W. Fowler, *Becoming Adult, Becoming Christian* (San Francisco: Harper and Row, 1984), p. 46.
64. See chapter by M. Jacobs, 'Is anatomy destiny?' in R. Holloway (ed.), *Who Needs Feminism? Male Responses to Sexism in the Church* (London: SPCK, 1991), pp. 149–60.
65. N. Golan, *Passing Through Transitions* (London: Collier Macmillan, 1981). Note also that Levinson was compelled by its shortcomings to follow his book: D. Levinson *et al.*, *The Seasons of a Man's Life* (New York: Knopf, 1978), with research into the seasons of women's lives, although he recognized that life 'follows an underlying universal pattern on which there are endless cultural and individual variations' (pp. 6–7).
66. Faber, pp. 275–7.
67. A. Vergote, *The Religious Man* (Dublin: Gill and Macmillan, 1969).
68. P. Turquet, 'Threats to Identity in the Large Group', in L. Kreeger (ed.), *The Large Group: Dynamics and Therapy* (London: Constable, 1975).
69. J. S. Dunne, *The Way of All the Earth: an Encounter with Eastern Religion* (London: Sheldon Press, 1973); *see also* his *The Reasons of the Heart* (London: SCM Press, 1978); and *Time and Myth*. I am intrigued to see that Kenneth Cracknell, in his chapter on inter-faith spirituality in *Towards a New Relationship* (Manchester: Epworth, 1986), also draws upon Keats and Dunne as I have done, to illustrate his own discipline. This synchronicity of thought (which is not in fact attributable to any of the conversations I have had with Kenneth Cracknell, since neither of us had mentioned either author) seems to

provide some confirmation of the appropriateness of this aspect of personal and faith maturity in relation to spirituality as well.

70. R. C. Zaehner, *Hinduism* (Oxford University Press, 1962), p. 186.

71. *The Independent*, 12 February 1993.

72. A. N. Wilson, *Against Religion*, Counterblast 19 (London: Chatto & Windus, 1991).

73. S. Freud, *One of the Difficulties of Psychoanalysis* (London: Hogarth Press, 1946), Collected Papers, 4, pp. 351-2.

74. H. Searles, *The Nonhuman Environment in Normal Development and in Schizophrenia* (New York: International Universities Press, 1960), p. 82.

75. Klein, p. 307.

76. Zaehner, p. 50.

77. D. Thomas, *Collected Poems 1934-1953*, ed. W. Davies and R. Maud, (London: Dent, 1988), p. 106.

78. F. Capra, *The Tao of Physics*, 3rd edn (London: HarperCollins, 1992), p. 50.

79. N. Mosley, *Hopeful Monsters* (London: Secker & Warburg, 1990), p. 29.

80. Capra, p. 336.

81. Shah, p. 85.

SIX

Complexity and Simplicity

Letting go

This study is approaching its end. But its finish, I need to repeat, is not the zenith of a psychology of belief, even if in this chapter I look at the 'heights' of experience. Neither is it a conclusion, because if there is one theme that runs throughout this final level of belief, it is that by its very nature illusions are 'beyond words' and even beyond images. I am aware of just how difficult it is 'at the end' to speak at all. Small wonder, in that strange visionary experience of John on Patmos, that when the seventh seal was opened 'there was silence in heaven about the space of half an hour'.[1] But my problem is more complicated still; it is like the riddle of one of the most famous *koans* asked of Zen pupils: 'How does one convey the sound of one hand clapping?'

Yet the theme of this chapter, if not the last illusion, has to be my last word in this context, because it sums up much that has gone before. In this chapter, the concerns of previous ones are extended and caught up in the common theme of 'letting go'. Written large here are aspects of letting go that have already been alluded to, such as: the realization of finitude, and recognition of the inevitability of death, albeit set confusingly in the context of the infinite; acknowledgement of common bonds with the natural world; the wish for integration and harmony with the universe, alongside concern for the oppressed and sacrifice of the self for the sake of the wider community; letting go of projections as essentially limited images and ideas; and passing beyond language to concepts that cannot be adequately expressed in any form.

It is tempting to get caught up in mystery and mystification because that is what many authors do when they describe these 'heights' of experience. In matters of belief and meaning, I have made it clear earlier that there is always a danger of idealization creeping in from the earliest levels of experience.

165

This ultimate stage of belief offers no excuse for such language or thinking: in Jungian terms, it is much more to do with deflation; in religious terms with humility; or in my terms with letting go, than it is with the respective opposites of inflation, sanctity and self-centredness.

Fowler requires a Stage to be distinctively different for it to warrant its own identity, yet the distinctiveness he gives Stage 6 is often to describe its constituent elements as being those of Stage 5 taken to an idealistic conclusion. I have considerable doubts, which I illustrate later, about Stage 6 as anything other than an extension of Stage 5, with the exception of a distinctive expression of thought used in some Western and much Eastern mysticism. The difficulties which other critics also have with Fowler's Stage 6 can be eased by dropping it as a separate Stage, or even a separate expression of belief, and by seeing it instead as a description of the direction in which Stage 5 people appear to be moving; or, like Kohlberg's 'stage 7', by regarding it as a metaphor for an ideal state. The only radically different aspect to this chapter, for instance, is in the letting go of language, which I examine in the final section; and even that is in some ways an extension of the poetic use of paradox which has already been present in Stage 5.

Fowler's idealization of his supposed Stage 6 is seen in the language he uses to describe it. He defines this stage as one where the division between vision and reality yields to 'radical actualization'. Although elsewhere he describes 'universalizing faith' as a comprehensive vision, with the absence of competition between faiths, Fowler betrays his definition in the final paragraphs of his study by elevating the Judaeo-Christian tradition as the culmination of experience.[2] That such a tradition itself takes many different forms is not addressed; which of the many forms of such a tradition is the greatest expression? Surely not them all? But even to ask this question is futile, demonstrating as it does that we have fallen into the same trap as Fowler of making comparisons. Like Watts' elevation of Zen Buddhism and Badcock's of psychoanalysis that I have mentioned in earlier chapters,[3] Fowler appears to follow those who would make hierarchy respectable: he may not use the phrase *primus inter pares* (first among equals), but that seems to be his conclusion!

Similarly, his choice of people who represent Stage 6 is not taken from the ordinary people of his research sample: they are nearly all 'Saints' from his own religious tradition. He lists as examples such people as Gandhi, Martin Luther King, Mother Teresa of Calcutta, Bonhoeffer, and Thomas Merton. Although Fowler concedes that he cannot simply list the renowned and that there must be many others who achieve this stage, he contradicts himself by describing this stage as 'extremely rare', again making it extremely precious and elitist.[4] In answer to criticism of the lack of any clear difference between Stage 5 and Stage 6 types of faith, Fowler argues that Stage 6 people are distinguished by the 'breakthrough of Spirit'; that up to the fifth Stage we see 'natural' development, but achievement of Stage 6 is through 'grace'.[5] Such singling out of Stage 6 people, as especially endowed with grace and the Spirit, smacks of the narrow exclusivity of some Stage 3 thinking.

The description of his Stage 6 examples oozes with unctuousness in the same way: he writes, for instance, of their 'redemptive subversiveness' and their 'relevant irrelevance', as though paradox (which he identifies elsewhere as a feature of Stage 5 faith) had gone to his head.[6] He mentions that many of those in this Stage die at the hands of those whom they hope to change; this is because while they liberate, they also threaten. Unintentionally, they show up the inconsistencies which exist in the rest of us. As Fowler states:

> They are more lucid, more simple, and yet somehow more fully human than the rest of us. They love life, but hold on to it loosely. They are ready for fellowship with people at any of the other Stages and from any other faith tradition, and the communities they seek to foster are inclusive of others too.[7]

Fowler qualifies his description of Stage 6 people by saying that they are neither perfect, nor fully 'actualized', and that they have their limitations. This is quite clear when hagiography is replaced by more realistic biography: Thomas Merton is one of Fowler's candidates for Stage 6, but Merton's official biographer makes clear a number of examples of Merton's self-centredness, even once he had attracted a huge and devoted following for his vision of the contemplative life, of world peace and of inter-faith understanding.[8] Erikson was very critical of certain of Gandhi's characteristics, finding it difficult at one stage to complete his psycho-biography.[9] I mean none of this as particular criticism of Merton or Gandhi; I cast doubt, rather, on the sanctifying process to which Fowler succumbs in seeking evidence for a Stage, which if it means anything at all, represents an ideal and little more.

Fowler loses his way in his eulogizing, not least because the premise of his language describes features I have already examined in Stage 5. There is nothing particularly new about this type of belief, except for the illustrious names he cites. Some of his description remains a helpful extension of the form of belief I set out in the last chapter, but treating Stage 6 as a separate state is misleading. There is, thank goodness, a simpler way of making room for the experience which he would otherwise make esoteric.

A simple example

Fowler cannot quite make up his mind as to whether 'universalizing faith' applies to an elite few or to many people. He might be spared this dilemma if he could see it as an experience of belief in action which is one part of the whole. Clearly, there are women and men who stand out in the history of world faiths as having lived at a particular level of spiritual experience more continuously than others have done; or who have acted upon their experience in more obviously courageous ways than others might appear to have done. But the type of spiritual experience which (as in Fowler's Stage 6) is frequently reserved for 'the elect', 'the Saints' and 'the mystics' is one that many others know in part, whether they are artists and artisans, scientists and civil servants, or (in Auden's phrase) poets and polytheists.[10] It is the nature rather than the extent of this type of belief that distinguishes this level of experience, making it a more intense form of levels of belief otherwise to be associated with Fowler's Stage 5 or with Tillich's world-view C.

The nature of such experience is beautifully described in one of the encounters recorded by Coles in his study of *The Spiritual Life of Children*. It is perhaps significant that he only records two examples of visionary experience in children, since such levels of belief and expression of belief are indeed rare at such an early age. But it is equally significant, given the argument that chronological age cannot be equated with

stages of belief, that his most telling illustration is an eight-
year-old girl. She is a Hopi Indian living in New Mexico. Hers
is an example of what we can only call (in the language of
paradox) profound simplicity, more expressive than much of
the high-flown language of scholars and interpreters. Fortunately Coles lets her speak for herself, and I would wish to do
the same, except I do not have the same opportunity here to
reproduce all the material: inevitably I have to summarize
and point the reader to the original text.[11]

Natalie was close to her own people, and much that she
expressed came from her Hopi tradition, although Coles
attributes her vision to 'an amalgam told by elders and a
child's embellishment of them, her private journey'.[12] It is her
own experience of the tradition which impresses, since it
could not simply have come from being taught it. Such ways
of seeing are not taught, even if they may to some extent be
'caught'. Coles describes her mind as 'almost lost in thought,
so engrossed was she with the land and the sky, the sun,
moon and stars, the flowers her mother grew, the animals,
the changes of light that came with clouds'. Coles describes
how they started their meeting by sitting in silence, watching
two hawks, which then flew away. They started to talk, but
Natalie knew when they had returned, even though she had
her back to them. Such was her feeling for the world in which
she lived, the first sign of how deeply in tune she was with
her environment.

The hawks provided the way into further conversation.
Natalie described to Coles how she met her ancestors in her
thoughts, and how 'we become birds when we die'. Her
ancestors lived in the *mesa* (table-land) which she and Coles
could see across the desert. 'We were put there so we could
always see for miles and miles, and we'd be nearer to the
clouds and the sun and the stars and the moon.' Natalie
described how she talked to her ancestors, how she saw
them, and how her thoughts were like the birds 'they rise and
circle and circle, and then they gradually head for the *mesa*
and our ancestors wait there for news of us'.

Thankfully, Coles realizes that Natalie is not psychotic—he
understands that her vivid language is metaphorical. But
neither does he get caught on a reductionist explanation that
her stories simply exhibit 'magical thinking'. Neither, in
Tillich's terms, are they examples of literal belief, since Natalie

gives cogent explanation of her experience. Coles writes of his reaction: 'I was taken by her simplicity, her lack of pretentiousness, her apparent lack of interest in whether her visions were credible by my psychological or cultural standards'. He encouraged her to tell him about what she saw. Natalie went on: 'The Hopis are there on the *mesa*, their spirits. Each spirit is a soul. You can't see them, not the way you see me and I see you. But they are there—and when we go there, we sit, and they talk to us'. There is no magical thinking or anthropomorphic projection here, because Natalie knows that talking with the spirits is different from her conversation with Coles. A little later she speaks of her 'day-dream' (informed by Hopi tradition) of the time when,

> All of us are together, and the waters of the rivers are full, and the sun has warmed the cold part of the world . . . That's when all the spirits will dance and dance, and the stars will dance, and the sun and the moon will dance, and the birds will swoop down and they'll dance, and all the people, everywhere, will stand up and dance, and then they'll sit down again in a big circle, so huge you can't see where it goes . . . No more fights. Fights are a sign that we have gotten lost, and forgotten our ancestors, and are in the worst trouble . . . And the whole world will be good when we're all in our big, big circle. We're going around and around until we all get to be there!

Her vision (like the vision of universal harmony in other faiths) is of 'an ultimate circular harmony [Coles' description]' embracing everyone, not just the Hopis.

Coles comments that Natalie shook her head when he asked her about God, because the Hopi are not comfortable with that word. She preferred the word 'spirit', meaning 'the collective spirit of her Hopi ancestors, the particular spirit that was hers, that was the dog Blackie's. Coles notes that he nearly wrote: '*her* dog Blackie's', but that would be out of keeping with her spirit and Blackie's since the Hopis are not (again in Cole's description): 'possessive so much as eager to be possessed. Her body is not an owner of what she regards as the spirit, now housed there. Her body is a link in a chain of life, even as all those links are part of a universe of life'.[13] Coles then asked Natalie what she meant by the 'spirit' she often mentioned. Natalie clearly thought hard, and there was silence. His account goes on, in a passage I must quote almost in full:

> Suddenly she stood up; so did Blackie. Natalie walked a few steps away from where we were sitting . . . She looked up at the sky. The dog looked up at her—she is Blackie's sky. Abruptly, Natalie raised her right arm and whirled it around and around, making circle after circle—a discus thrower, I thought, readying for a climactic heave; and then *it*, the last big exertion. The dog didn't wait. Blackie knew. She was off and running, furiously running . . . pursuing some mirage or other. In about fifteen or twenty seconds, Blackie stopped, faced about, looked at Natalie, started running towards her, kneeled at her feet, received an affectionate hug, and heard the words 'thank you'.
>
> What did this pantomime have to do with what had been (or so I thought) an attempt at rational discussion? When Natalie returned to her chair she was quick to help me out:
>
> 'The "spirit" is when you go running for someone. It is when you try to send signals to someone. It is when you are being as much you as you can be. When Blackie ran, her spirit was there for me and you to see! When I used my arm with her, it was my spirit talking to her spirit!'

I have drawn upon this conversation with Natalie at length because it contains a visionary quality; and in the attempt to put this into words, it expresses much of what Fowler would wish to include in Stage 5 or 6, but is untarnished by idealization or pretentiousness. In Fowler's linear model, it might be difficult to find a place for Natalie other than in the Stages of magical and mythical thinking, although Coles is astute enough to know that such a description is not sufficient. By using the more fluid model that I have been adopting throughout this study, Natalie's visionary or mystical experience need not be limited to age or to a developmental stage. If Stage 6 is to be described as 'universalizing faith' it needs also to be seen as in some respects a universal experience, albeit in most people an occasional one which from time to time transcends their usual levels of belief. Coles recognizes Natalie's experience as unusual in one so young, but also unusual in her willingness to try and convey, as graphically as she did, what she believed. Not only does she 'see' and 'experience', she also translates—like the artist and the poet, or Capra's physicist at the third stage of research, she shows the ability to use an alternative formulation in order to communicate with others 'in plain language'. This is 'a criterion of the understanding they have reached'.[14]

Natalie's expression of belief includes most of the areas which constitute the theme of 'letting go'. In line with the sections that follow, her vision includes aspects of relinquishment of the self, self-sacrifice and concern for the whole community, mystical and visionary experience and the limits of language.

Relinquishing the self

I have suggested many times already that the themes which dominate growth and development cannot be restricted to one age. Although letting go is a central feature of this expression of belief, the process has already been present from birth itself. Later on, it is also seen in the toddler letting go a parent's hand, an example of the many separations that accompany different stages of life. Equally, I do not forget, as I have observed in earlier places, that different forms of belief develop as alternative ways of dealing with existential anxiety, which ultimately is about facing the final separation in death. Letting go at death is often just as much a psychological act as it is a physical one; as the old rite of commendation recognizes, almost commanding the 'soul' to 'go forth upon your journey from this world . . .'.[15] Dying is an active process, reflected in the opening words Winnicott wrote in a journal he kept when he knew he was going to die from a lung disease: 'Prayer: O God, may I be alive when I die'.[16]

Erikson includes 'renunciation' as one of the strengths of old age. Religion has made much of renunciation too, although sometimes it appears as an overprotective defence against sexuality and the fulfilment of other personal needs and desires, very different from the Zen principle of 'eat when you are hungry, sleep when you are tired'.[17] Nevertheless, it is in relation to others that renunciation of the self can play a positive role in promoting active concern. Fowler includes lack of self-concern as one of the marks of maturity, which according to his model makes its first appearance in Stage 5. This appears a contentious statement, since selflessness and concern for others appears in children as well as in conformist adults. What Fowler is trying to convey is that it is only at this later point that there is genuine altruism. In childhood, the apparently selfless act helps preserve the good aspects of relationships; and in conformist adulthood, it may be because it is socially expected. Kohlberg's early and middle levels of moral thinking also apply here. Fowler links lack of self-concern in Stage 5 to readiness for martyrdom in Stage 6, as I examine in the next section.

Motivation is notoriously difficult to measure. Altruism or self-interest is impossible to judge. What is more helpful is the parallel drawn by Fingarette between psychoanalysis and mysticism in relation to self-concern. He examines the possibility of a link between an ideal state of psychological maturity, and ideal faith: neither can ever be achieved, but such positions can be envisaged. He compares the faith of the mystics, and their wish to attain perfect union with the divine, and psychoanalysis and the ideal of state of being 'fully analysed'.[18] He does not assume that either can ever be achieved, but they have in common a goal which (together with the better parts of Fowler's Stage 6) is worth aiming at.[19]

Fingarette compares the hypothetical outcome of successful psychoanalysis with the height of mystical experience. One feature that they share is the paradox that, in becoming more self conscious, both the analysand and the mystic cease to be so concerned about themselves. To different degrees, most of us are 'compulsive, obsessive, acutely self-conscious, focusing . . . attention upon our feelings and our perceptions, our theoretical distinctions and logical proofs'.[20] Letting go of the self, Fingarette suggests, does not involve self-negation as such, but being able to let go of a particularly anxious form of self-consciousness. It is this which is involved in the way of enlightenment. He draws more heavily upon Eastern than upon Western mysticism to illustrate his argument. But enlightenment does not mean the loss of 'sensing, perceiving, thinking, discriminating [which] are essential functions within the enlightened life'. These qualities are very similar to the four personality types proposed by Jungian psychology, where maturation and individuation include integration of the thinking, feeling, intuitive and sensing parts of the personality. These 'merge so that a person's conscious attitudes, and hence a greater part of his experience of himself, will become richer and more variegated'.[21]

Fingarette gives different illustrations of how a person who has experienced the benefits of psychoanalysis to the full also shows some of the characteristics of the mystic. In 'not being concerned' about the self, such people do not feel angry for themselves, or do not get upset easily if other people say things that are intended to hurt. The self (in the sense of self-image perhaps) has been sufficiently integrated to let go of self-concern, so that it does not matter what other people think or say. This does not imply that analysis, any more than mystic experience, leads to a person being withdrawn, or cool, as if they 'couldn't care less. He or she enjoys life, but is not dependent upon it. There is in both the mystic and the analysed person intense participation, warmth, and the ability to feel, but without self-concern'.[22]

Terms such as integration and integrity, individuation and maturity have already formed part of the description of belief in the last chapter. There is nothing new about what Fingarette is describing, except that it is clear that such perception has moved beyond the self-absorption in inner experience which is one of the limiting factors of those levels of belief. Despite using 'ideal' experiences, Fingarette makes rather more accessible and identifiable than Fowler's list of 'Saints', how in more limited visionary experience, or in less than complete therapy, 'ordinary' people can be gradually freed from self-concern. This is quite different from a self that is to be denied or negated, as a superficial reading of the mystics (or indeed Freud, with his reality principle) might have us believe.

Guntrip expresses the relationship between self and lack of self-concern well when he writes: 'The peak of maturity . . . [is] to be able to give oneself to the utmost in love, for convincing reasons, without loss of ego-integrity'.[23] Personal development, particularly in these later stages, leads to lessening of the three basic forms of existential anxiety as described in Tillich's analysis: anxiety about death, anxiety about emptiness and anxiety about guilt.[24] The move away from the secondary narcissism of young adulthood (and of Fowler's Stage 4) is helped by the growing realization in the second half of life of the inevitability of death, leading to less anxiety about fate or death in those who experience 'conjunctive' and 'universalizing faith'. At this level of experience, where the search for meaning is enriched by the wisdom of one's own and of other faiths, a person begins to replenish the vacuum of emptiness and loss of meaning that earlier conventional beliefs in the end failed to satisfy. Finally, the deeper self-analysis that forms part of the movement towards individuation and integrity, helps a person to let go of the sterile preoccupation with guilt and condemnation, and achieve deeper self-knowledge and fuller self-confidence. This leads in turn (again in Tillich's terms) to the courage to be oneself, the courage to be a full participant in the community and in the world, and — pointing forward to my conclusion — the courage to be rooted in what Tillich calls 'the God above God'.[25]

Self-sacrifice and political concern

In his attempt to distinguish a Stage 6, Fowler makes great play of the apparent shift in concern from self-interest, through social action, to losing one's life for one's beliefs. There is a danger, referred to in the last chapter, that Stage 5 interest in stories and images (and we might add in poetic, artistic and scientific expression) gives rise to a type of paralysis of action, as people in this Stage find themselves caught between their vision and reality. They may dream of a fairer world, of the common joys and sorrows that unite the peoples of the world (as Natalie the Hopi Indian did), but Stage 5, even when such visions are translated into activity, is one which remains paradoxical and divided (according to Fowler), 'because the self is caught between universalizing apprehensions and the need to preserve its own being and well-being'.[26] Added to this is the difficulty of coming to terms with the paradox of a vision of change on the one hand, and disillusion with the world's inability to change on the other (or, more accurately, with humanity's intransigence). Fowler suggests in his proposed Stage 6 that personal threat does not deter people from speaking out for change, often invoking non-violent strategies to achieve their vision. Fowler views those who are at this stage as less concerned with self-preservation, as exhibiting more transcendent moral and religious qualities. Their vision is of a universal community.

There are all manner of problems in such an analysis. By restricting himself to non-violent strategies, Fowler neatly excludes religious militants and fundamentalists, but they also have a vision of a perfect community — even if they employ a more violent means to achieve it. He makes a clear distinction between Stage 6 and fanaticism. Fanatical believers similarly have a vision, and they are not infrequently carried along by a religious community that wishes to unite the world in some form of eschatological paradise. They also demonstrate their willingness to die for the cause; but the fanatic, and the fanatical community, seeks unity and the fulfilment of vision on the basis of forcing others to conform, and not on the basis of freedom and love. Nevertheless, his distinctions are not clear enough to rule out non-violence or even forms of moral blackmail from being used for selfish ends; or violence sometimes being necessary as an inevitable outcome of the pursuit of a greater good. These ethical issues about means and ends are not as simple as Fowler's definition makes them appear. Furthermore, self-sacrifice can be made in the service of futility — the Great War and Vietnam provide horrifying examples.

Another objection is that, although some men and women may provide an example and take the lead, self-sacrifice is involved in following them as well: it was not just Gandhi or Martin Luther King who lost their lives for their respective visions of independence or integration in their societies. Those whom they represent as figureheads are equally prepared to renounce their own lives for the sake of their dream. None of the great revolutionaries (whether in religion or politics) succeeded on their own, but because they represented a body of people who shared the same ideals and values.

Remove the element of martyrdom, which is further evidence of Fowler's pre-occupation with a book of Saints, and letting go of the self can then be extended from its beginnings in the early stages of faith, through the lessening of self-concern in the later levels of belief, to being ready to lose one's life for the sake of the 'truth' (illusory though the truth inevitably is). This level of belief, translated into action (or inaction) includes those with their head in the clouds at one end of the spectrum, and those whose blood soaks into the earth at the other.

Fowler reminds us that it is misleading to think of those who have intense spiritual experiences as necessarily having their heads in the clouds. Leech rightly observes, in terms that reflect the theme of this book, that authentic mysticism involves 'a confrontation with all forms of illusion and pretence within our own persons and in our society. The mystical way is essentially subversive . . . the *via negativa* has profound political implications'.[27] In recognizing the potentially subversive nature of mysticism, Leech uses the same phrase as Fowler does in describing Stage 6 people as 'subversive of the structures (including religious structures) by which we sustain our corporate survival, security and significance'.[28]

Mystical experience

The last chapter reintroduced, in a more expressive form, the wonder at and sense of affinity with nature which is found in children and many less industrialized communities. In discussing the non-human environment in particular, it was clear that many people have experiences of a sublime and spiritual nature, which are not specifically related to religion, but more to the world in which we 'live and move and have our being'.[29] Such sublime moments are found in abundance in poetry and music, when it feels as if 'the whole world is charged with the grandeur of God'.[30]

Winnicott describes the experience of ecstasy as an 'ego-orgasm': 'In the normal person, a highly satisfactory experience such as may be obtained at a concert or at the theatre or in a friendship may deserve such a term . . . which draws attention to the climax and the importance of the climax'. It is important to recognize that Winnicott distinguishes this from sex. 'In my opinion, if we compare the happy play of a child or the experience of an adult at a concert with a sexual experience, the difference is so great that we should do no harm in allowing a different term for the description of the two experiences.'[31] Such a distinction is valuable to have in mind, although the erotic element of mystical experience can also be sublimely sexual, as vividly portrayed in Bernini's statue of the *Ecstasy of St. Teresa*, which Clark calls 'one of the most deeply moving works in European art'. Bernini captures in flowing marble the supreme moment of the piercing love of God the Saint herself describes: 'The pain was so great that I screamed aloud, but simultaneously felt such infinite sweetness that I wished the pain to last eternally. It was the sweetest caressing of the soul by God'.[32]

It is clear that these experiences, whether in the mystic's vision, in the play of a child or in the ego-orgasm of an audience at a concert, do not arise from conscious acts of will: they come, to use a metaphor, 'out of the blue'. Experience of the transcendent (or, remembering Winnicott's phrase, 'transitional space') cannot simply be gained by seeking after it. Such experience breaks in from outside (is that perhaps what Fowler means by 'grace'?), although quite what the 'outside' is, and whether the outside is not inside, are questions which cannot and need not be answered at this level of belief. Fingarette equates psychoanalytic insight with mystic experience as being passively received, in this case from a person's own consciousness (or better, the unconscious) rather than something that is actively produced or deliberately searched for.[33] The Christian mystics warn against the seduction of seeking trances and visions. Perhaps the most apt image for such experience is 'the hound of heaven',[34] reminding us that the transcendent breaks through at the point we cease either to flee from it or even to chase it.

Such experiences are much more common than Fowler's rarified Stage 6 presumes. These moments come and are soon gone, and we are often left as much in the dark as before, although at the same time we know we have caught a glimpse of something out of the ordinary. It is like walking in the country on a pitch black and stormy night, when a flash of lightning unforgettably and briefly lights up our surroundings, and leaves us as quickly as it came. We are not able to 'see' our way forward any better with our eyes than we were before; but we are left with a mental picture that guides our path, just for a while.

The traditional, religious view is to see union with God as the pinnacle of experience and therefore of spiritual maturity. Part of the problem with such a statement is that such heights of experience cannot be put adequately into words. When they are, poetic descriptions sometimes give the impression that these unique experiences are only open to the relatively few; hence perhaps the attraction of the mystic experience to Fowler as a mark of Stage 6 faith. Remove the esotericism of this Stage, and the experience becomes more recognizable in other people, in many different forms, in religious experience, as well as through the stimulus of other forms of thought and expression in art and science. In relation to science, both Capra in *The Tao of Physics* and Zohar in *The Quantum Self* separately draw upon quantum theory as their inspiration and insight. Zohar's argument, for example, is that quantum physics allied to a quantum model of consciousness provides a perspective for seeing ourselves as part of each other and part of the universe as a whole. Such a perspective would not 'replace all the vast poetic and mythological imagery, the spiritual and moral dimensions of religion, but it would provide us with the physical basis for a coherent world picture'.[35] Capra points to features of mystical experience when he describes a scientist's insight as tending to come 'not when sitting at a desk working out the equations, but when relaxing, in the bath, during a walk in the wood . . . The intuitive mind seems to take over and can produce the sudden clarifying insights which give so much joy and delight to scientific research'.[36] What is relatively rare is the ability to express such experiences, although such an ability is not confined to the intellectually gifted and the artistically skilled. Natalie showed an equal capacity to do the same in her moving enactment of the 'spirit'.

But what is involved in this heightened sense: union with God, with nature or with fellow men and women? Freud suggests that the desire for spiritual bliss is a wish for the return of the oceanic feelings of childhood, originally experienced in the symbiotic mother-baby relationship. Jung sees the same experience as related to the collective unconscious and archetypes. Both Freud and Jung have been criticized by Wilber, a transpersonal psychologist: Freud, for reducing the transcendent to the pre-personal; and Jung, for elevating everything from the pre-personal to the transcendent. I do not propose to introduce yet another model of development, as proposed by Wilber, especially as many of his stages show considerable overlap with models which I have already employed.[37] What is more important to observe is the particular emphasis which transpersonal psychology (which Wilber represents) gives to the dynamic relationship between the personal (the first four stages in Wilber's model) and the transpersonal. Wilber argues the need to transcend ego-psychology and to grow into harmony with the 'transcendent Being of the Universe'. His fifth stage has similarities with Fowler's Stage 5, since it moves beyond the ego to a more panoramic vision, towards deep integrity, towards archetypes (as in Jung's psychology), towards transcendent awareness, and towards the source and ground of all structures. Wilber's sixth stage is that of 'Spirit', 'pure Being' and 'God'.

What is particularly pertinent to this study is Wilber's assertion that union with the transcendent is not the same as the primary symbiotic unity of infancy. The state of the infant is one of ignorance, so that she cannot yet be one with the world, whether it is the personal world or the symbolic world. We must not confuse the all-embracing microcosm of the infant with the vastness of the universe as we begin to realize it in adult life.[38] Fingarette might agree, since he quotes Meister Eckhart with approval: 'One must achieve this unself-consciousness by means of transformed knowledge. *This* ignorance does not come from lack of self-knowledge but rather it is from knowledge that one may achieve this ignorance'.[39] Watts expresses the same idea in quoting the Zen parable that those who know nothing of Zen think that mountains are mountains, trees are trees and men are men. Those who study Zen begin to see how mountains, trees and men are only transient appearances (illusions) with no abiding reality. But those who have a full understanding of Zen once again see mountains as mountains, trees as trees and men as men.[40] T. S. Eliot's much quoted phrase puts it in poetic form, and indeed *The Four Quartets* expresses in both ideas and language much of what this chapter tries to convey in more prosaic words:

> And the end of all our exploring
> Will be to arrive where we started
> And know the place for the first time.[41]

A similar link between first and last stages, the beginning and the end, is made by Erikson when he writes that 'where adults have integrity enough not to fear death, their children will not fear life'.[42] Perhaps the wisdom which Erikson associates with old age, comes about partly through the second virtue which he includes in that period of life — renunciation, the ability to let go, including the willingness to let go of the purely rational as the sole way of knowing.

Fingarette distinguishes between the naïvety of a child, and the humility of the person who has learned from life experience. To this difference could be added that a child's sense of unity is accompanied by an omnipotent sense of the world being part of the child, whereas in mature adults this unity is experienced as the self being part of the world (or of the transcendent). Such distinctions are important and relevant, because there is clearly in many respects a similarity between the transcendent experiences that are part of the expression of belief in the Stages of 'conjunctive' and 'universalizing faith', and the 'blooming, buzzing confusion' of Stage 0, 'primal faith'. It is equally apparent in injunctions requiring the simplicity of a child to enter the kingdom of heaven, that a close parallel must be drawn between the true belief of an adult and the faith of a child. But, unlike Wilber, Fingarette prefers to view the loss of self in unity with God — or 'the One' in Eastern mysticism — as a definite regression to childhood. He believes that it is an experience of natural creative regression, just as going back to infancy is part of therapy itself.[43] The psychoanalytic belief in the self-regulation of the ego requires a person to go back to beginnings in order to develop. There is, therefore, every justification for the mystic who reaches to the heights of maturity, like the mythical 'fully analysed patient', to regress more in order to develop more. I showed in Chapter 3 how Erikson attached much the same positive value to a return to the maternal matrix.[44]

An interesting example of this same dilemma, whether what is 'at the end' is also 'at the beginning' and the relationship between the two poles of experience, is found in the reaction of different critics to the contemporary composer John Tavener. His music illustrates the identification and yet the distinction between the simplicity of early processes and the complexity of mature thought and experience. John Tavener's work is deeply embedded in the tradition of Eastern (and Russian) Orthodox music. One article described his music as:

> A consciously conservative yearning — this return to the sacred roots, this love of unbroken tradition, this pastoral nostalgia . . . simplicity has become his deepest aesthetic . . . This simplicity, in particular his music's quality of wavering, radiant premonition — as if it is always about to reveal a glory too large for it to express — is deeply seductive . . . One can only long for more simplicity, more self-extinction.[45]

Notice the way in which the different aspects of the theme of letting go are found in this passage. It is perhaps significant that, in the article just quoted, Tavener is himself described as having a faith which tends towards the self-dissolution of the *via negativa* (see later), and that all those who know him speak of him as 'wonderfully free from arrogance or self-importance'. It is as if the music reflects the person, and the person the music, although, from what Tavener says about the need to keep psychology out of music, I suspect that he might disagree with such a close identification.

The same article also reflects a diametrically opposite re-action to Tavener's music, which is equally important to my argument at this point. It is clearly experienced by others, including other composers, as being *too* simple. One musician is quoted as saying: 'It's a lovely sound but it's so simple. What does it have to offer the musically literate? Every parameter has been drastically limited, so that what you have is ritual—repetitive simplicity. I think it's substitute religion'. Another says: 'I fear that it's essentially a private ritual'. The contradictory ways of interpreting Tavener's music are summed up in the article: 'Tavener's restoration of that sacred music may be the end of a cycle—a terminus—or it may represent a beginning. We shall see.' The paradox reflected in the juxtaposition of both these ways of looking at his music suggests the impossibility of ever knowing whether what appears simple in any sphere of thought or artistic expression is a return to childhood or the mark of genuine maturity; whether simplicity is a regressive flight to memories of a past where little gave rise to anxiety or conflict, or whether simplicity is the only way of meeting the challenge of paradox head on. Perhaps daring to give expression to the essential contradictions of life's experience which have dogged us from birth (in a way which at first sight appears disarmingly simplistic), later yields insights into complexities which can (and indeed should) never be resolved.

The limits of language

In describing the broadening and deepening of experience of other faiths and forms of expression in the last chapter, I illustrated how such a level of belief moves away from slavish dependency upon narrow interpretations of faith (whether at conformist Stage 3 or reductive Stage 4) so that the imagination is capable of embracing 'all kinds of other ideas and aspirations and hopes, things that are to be loved and worshipped'.[46] Once access has been gained by this opening of the windows of the mind, there is an inexhaustible treasury of beauty and savagery, wisdom and humour, and stimulus and comfort—which some will find in religion, others in art, music or literature, and others in nature or in the scientific quest. These treasures are open to many interpretations.

Yet there is also considerable evidence, especially in the literature that comes from different world faiths, which suggests that there are experiences where the language of poetry and metaphor are insufficient, or the images and symbols of art and science fail. Language is still used: but only through negation is it possible to approximate to what the illusion tries to convey. Despite their limitations, words prove paradoxically to be capable of enriching understanding. This is paradox carried through to its ultimate. Shah describes the Sufi use of 'enciphered material—not designed especially or always to conceal a real meaning, but intended to show, when decoded, that what on its outward face seemed like a complete poem, myth, treatise and so on, is susceptible of another interpretation: a sort of demonstration analagous to a kaleidoscopic effect'.[47]

It is at this point that I am anxious that words do not fail me in trying to decode, with some sufficient simplicity, the complexity of certain levels of experience. The problem is that, however simple, the words do not in themselves convey the actual experience. Indeed, the words and phrases that I use as illustrations are so simple that they appear to mean nothing, when they are intended to convey a complex of ideas. The reader may therefore understand the concept of paradox and negation, but might still be unable to enter the experience which my examples suggest. Any attempt to understand this final aspect of belief depends less upon intellectual comprehension, and more upon 'seeing through' the words and phrases, as much as in other moments of 'insight'. Sufis state there is a form of knowledge which 'is to scholastic learning as adulthood is to infancy'.[48] Although words do not fail completely, they make more sense when a person has had a similar experience. Fingarette observes that the problem of describing experience is as real for the psychoanalytic patient as it is for the mystic, since it 'involves a peculiar shifting of mental gears'.[49]

The particular aspect of belief that I am describing here is letting go of illusion or, in more prosaic terms: the negation of God, religion and faith. This is an important, if neglected, part of the Western mystical tradition. In his extensive survey of spiritual theology Leech makes only one reference to the *via negativa*, although it is an important one.[50] I have already cited earlier Leech's concurrence that the mystical experience includes 'a confrontation with all forms of illusion and pretence. The mystical way is essentially subversive . . . the *via negativa* has profound political implications'. It is, as I illustrate later, more fully expressed in Eastern religions. When a wise man in the *Upanishads* is asked to define God, he is silent; meaning that God is silence. When asked to describe God in words, he says 'Not this, not this'.[51] The *via negativa* — the way of negation — involves emptying the mind of the limitations of language and intellectual knowledge. All language about God has to be in the negative: God is *not* this and *not* that; even, in the words of the pseudonymous mystic Dionysius, 'God is not God'. This is the ultimate, and most difficult, act of relinquishment, as hard as death. There appears to be a stage of insight, enlightenment, vision, or as the unknown English mediaeval mystic puts it, of 'unknowing' which as one writer suggests, has moved beyond (for example) the imagery of Ignatian spirituality or Jungian individuation or the language of poetry.[52] Jones believes that Jung, in particular, needs the *via negativa* to 'slow him down', and suggests that greater understanding of the *via negativa* comes from Freud's explanation of religion as illusion, for which he provided clinical evidence and explanation.[53] A Freudian view of religion perhaps urges a pure form of faith, free from illusion, consonant with the highest points of religious thought. We come full circle, to the point at which we began in the opening pages of this book.

Freud's explanation of God and of much religious imagery, to recall Chapter 1, was that we transfer and project on to God experiences, fantasies and fears primarily related to parents and other significant figures from childhood. Transference analysis, which includes analysis of the language we use about God, is similar to the understanding of the fourth and fifth century desert hermits, who seem to have known that there was transference and projection (without using such technical terms) in some of the images and visions that they experienced. It was for this reason that they cultivated the negation of such images and visions, to arrive at a more pure form of experience. Jones sees certain patterns in common between the psychoanalytic process and the *via negativa* of the desert fathers. Amongst the parallels are: the need for detachment; the belief that nothing is accidental; the assertion that we are not as free as we like to think we are; the value of remembering, as an important part of growth; the conviction that, while much of what we do has to be done alone, companionship is essential; the necessity for contemplative commitment; an appreciation of our fallenness; and (especially pertinent at this point) the mystery of having to let go of the things and the people we love the most. This also means letting go our language—including our intellectual perceptions about God, faith, and all the other expressions of illusion which I have included in this study. Showing his surrealist heritage, the French analyst Lacan wrote: 'For what we have in the discovery of psycho-analysis is an encounter, an essential encounter—a *rendez-vous* to which we are always called with a real that eludes us'.[54]

By now, this position is not a new one to the reader: it draws upon Freud's reductive analysis of projections and transference, upon Winnicott's affirmation of the value of disillusionment, and upon Cupitt's analysis of theological patterns of thought. Indeed, the use of human and earthly images to tolerate the anxiety of being alone, or the inability to make sense of experience, and their use as 'transitional objects' is more than a psychological observation. It is also clear from a study of theology (though much less accepted and acted upon in arguments about credal statements, in the conduct of ritual and liturgy, or in pastoral ministry) that, although theologians may differ in their explanations and descriptions of God, they are ultimately forced into a common position that all their language about God is metaphorical. Some theologians make this explicit, as in Tillich's phrase 'God above God', or in Bonhoeffer's 'religionless Christianity'. When God is portrayed as 'Father' (or 'Mother') or even by a less personalized image, or when God is given qualities normally understood as applying to ordinary human relationships, all such descriptions are both limited and limiting.

Psychoanalytic and theological thinking equally understand language as having a transitional quality. In religious contexts, where God-talk is so much part of the stock-in-trade, it is especially easy to forget that 'prophecies, tongues and knowledge fail' as much as they ever did in the sectarian community at Corinth.55 No wonder the Hopi Indian girl did not like the word 'God'. Many people who are unused to God-talk, like the little boy who declares the Emperor has no clothes, see its flaws more obviously.

> The end of religion . . . is God. Contrariwise, God is the end of religion in the sense that once He appears vividly before us, in His depth and love and unrelenting truth, all else dissolves, or at the least religious paraphernalia drop back into their due and mundane place, and the concept 'religion' is brought to an end.56

I am sure that these words of Cantwell Smith's will be interpreted in as many ways as there are readers of them. For some people, the end of religion is a vision of a personal God. Whether it is that they have no need of an alternative end, or whether their imagination can grasp no other I do not know. If it is for them sufficient, and if they do not seek to compel me to think differently for myself, so be it. For me, when I am able to contemplate at this level of abstraction and negation, the end of religion means that all our language, all our symbols, all our churches and other religious communities, all our doctrines and creeds need to disappear before the immensity of the concept of the transcendent. Eastern and Western faith provide confirmation:

> Right views are called 'transcendental',
> Erroneous views are called 'worldly',
> But when all views, both right and erroneous, are
>   discarded.
> Then the essence of Wisdom manifests itself. (Buddhist)57

> For our knowledge and our prophecy alike are partial, and the partial vanishes when wholeness comes. (Christian)58

> Until college and minaret have crumbled
> This holy work of ours will not be done.
> Until faith becomes rejection, and rejection becomes belief
> There will be no true Muslim. (Sufi)59

I pray God to rid me of God. The highest and loftiest thing that one can let go of is to let go of God for the sake of God.[60]

The source of this last quotation is Meister Eckhart. I hesitate to call him 'Christian' since the mediaeval church, showing its conventional institutional wisdom, declared him a heretic and condemned his writings. Those who have achieved some kind of enlightenment are frequently seen as strange or different, and become outcasts. In the Sufi tradition there is a saying: 'None attains to the Degree of Truth until a thousand honest people have testified that he is a heretic'.[61]

Conclusion

This expression of belief supports the linking of wisdom and renunciation in Erikson's descriptions of the two 'virtues' most appropriate to mature adulthood. Renunciation and negation may seem a strange note upon which to finish a book which, like all writing, uses the medium of words, metaphor, and concrete ideas. Such thinking (or more accurately, 'unthinking') is difficult to sustain for long, and no doubt like many of my readers, I prefer the security and colour of images, even if I do not thirst after facts. I have been tempted, throughout this last chapter, to try and gather in as many different expressions of this level of belief, in order to demonstrate for all to see the essential unity of diverse patterns of discourse, of intellectual disciplines, of artistic and cultural expression and of faith. I had to stop myself, and ask what the nature of the illusion was that I was trying to create. Was I being drawn again into the illusion of primal unity? And why? To make the ending neat and comfortable? What of the final disillusion and dissolution? Do the complexities of all these levels and experiences of belief make it too simple to say there may be nothing there?

Notes

1. Revelation 8. 1.
2. J. W. Fowler, *Stages of Faith: the Psychology of Human Development and the Quest for Meaning* (San Francisco: Harper and Row, 1981), pp. 204–11.

3. A. Watts, *The Spirit of Zen* (London: HarperCollins, 1991), p. 40; C. R. Badcock, *The Psychoanalysis of Culture* (Oxford: Blackwell, 1980), p. 247.
4. Fowler, *Stages of Faith*, p. 200.
5. J. W. Fowler, *Becoming Adult, Becoming Christian* (San Francisco: Harper and Row, 1984), pp. 72-4.
6. Fowler, *Stages of Faith*, pp. 200-1.
7. In *Stages of Faith* (1981) Fowler includes communities of Stage 6 faith (p. 201), even though he omits them in his *Faith Development and Pastoral Care* (Philadelphia: Fortress Press, 1987).
8. M. Mott, *The Seven Mountains of Thomas Merton* (London: Sheldon Press, 1986).
9. E. Erikson, *Gandhi's Truth* (New York: Norton, 1969).
10. Cited by K. Cracknell, *Towards a New Relationship* (Manchester: Epworth Press, 1986), p. 143.
11. R. Coles, *The Spiritual Life of Children* (London: HarperCollins, 1992), pp. 148-58. The references in the paragraphs below all come from this section of his book.
12. Coles, p. 155.
13. Coles, p. 156.
14. F. Capra, *The Tao of Physics*, 3rd edn (London: HarperCollins, 1992), p. 38.
15. Ministry to the Sick, *Authorized Alternative Services* (London: SPCK, 1983), p. 37. For fuller treatment of the subject, *see also* P. Speck and I. Ainsworth-Smith, *Letting Go: Caring for the Dying and Bereaved* (London: SPCK, 1982).
16. I do not have a reference for this, although I have seen the quotation in print.
17. Quoted by Watts, p. 43.
18. Towards the very end of his life, Freud examined the impossibility of a complete analysis in a paper *Analysis Terminable and Interminable*, standard edn, vol. 23 (London: Hogarth Press).
19. H. Fingarette, *The Self in Transformation* (New York: Basic Books, 1963), p. 335.
20. Fingarette, p. 319.
21. A. Samuels, *Jung and the Post-Jungians* (London: Routledge and Kegan Paul, 1985), pp. 62-4.
22. Fingarette, p. 295.
23. H. Guntrip, *Psychoanalytic Theory, Therapy and the Self* (London: Hogarth Press, 1971), p. 124.
24. P. Tillich, *The Courage to Be* (New York: Nisbet, 1952), pp. 37-51.
25. Tillich, pp. 176-80.
26. Fowler, *Stages of Faith*, p. 200.
27. K. Leech, *True God* (London: Sheldon Press, 1985), p. 348.
28. Fowler, *Stages of Faith*, p. 201.
29. Acts 17. 28.
30. Gerard Manley Hopkins, 'God's Grandeur'.
31. D. W. Winnicott, *The Maturational Processes and the Facilitating Environment* (London: Hogarth Press, 1965), p. 35.

32. K. Clark, *Civilisation: a Personal View* (London: BBC Publications, 1969), p. 191.
33. Fingarette, p. 329.
34. Psalm 139. 7. The whole psalm expresses much that is relevant here, including the imagery of the womb and of infancy.
35. D. Zohar, *The Quantum Self* (London: HarperCollins, 1991), p. 201.
36. Capra, p. 39.
37. For a summary of Wilber's theory, see W. S. Schmidt, 'An Ontological Model of Development', *Journal of Pastoral Care*, Volume 40:1 (1986), pp. 56–67. He particularly cites K. Wilber, *Up from Eden: a Transpersonal View of Human Evolution* (New York: Anchor Press/ Doubleday, 1981).
38. Schmidt, p. 58.
39. Fingarette, p. 324.
40. Watts, p. 72.
41. T. S. Eliot, 'Little Gidding' from 'The Four Quartets'.
42. E. Erikson, *Childhood and Society* (London: Penguin Books, 1965), p. 261.
43. Fingarette, pp. 332–4.
44. E. Erikson, *Young Man Luther* (London: Faber & Faber, 1959), p. 257.
45. James Wood, 'Chant of the Mystic Musician', *Guardian*, 20 July 1992.
46. Cracknell, p. 143.
47. I. Shah, *The Way of the Sufi* (London: Penguin Books, 1974), p. 29.
48. Shah, p. 28.
49. Fingarette, pp. 327–30.
50. Leech, p. 348.
51. J. Mascaró, *The Upanishads* (London: Penguin Books, 1965), p. 12.
52. A. Jones, *Soul Making* (London: SCM Press, 1986).
53. S. Freud, 'A Question of a Weltanschauung' in *New Introductory Lectures on Psychoanalysis* (London: Penguin Freud Library), vol. 2, chapter 35.
54. J. Lacan, *Le Séminaire, Livre IX* (unpublished). Quoted by J. Forrester, *The Seductions of Psychoanalysis* (Cambridge University Press, 1990), p. 212. .
55. 1 Corinthians 13. 8.
56. W. Cantwell Smith, *The Meaning and End of Religion* (London: SPCK, 1978), p. 201; quoted by Cracknell, p. 191.
57. Fingarette, p. 323.
58. 1 Corinthians 13. 9. New English Bible version.
59. Shah, p. 48.
60. M. Fox, *Meditations with Eckhart* (Santa Fe: Bear and Co., 1983), p. 50.
61. Shah, p. 268.

Bibliography

Ashbrook, J. B., 'Review of "The Play of the Imagination: Toward a Psychoanalysis of Culture"', *Journal of Pastoral Care*, 39:2 (1985), p. 195.

Badcock, C. R., *The Psychoanalysis of Culture*, Oxford: Blackwell, 1980.

Baldridge, W. E. and Gleason, J. J., 'A Theological Framework for Pastoral Care', *Journal of Pastoral Care*, 32:4 (1978), pp. 232–8.

Balint, M., *The Basic Fault*, Tavistock Publications, 1968.

Belotti, E., *Little Girls*, London: Readers and Writers Co-operative, 1985.

Bettelheim, B., *The Uses of Enchantment*, London: Penguin Books, 1978.

Bettelheim, B., *Freud and Man's Soul*, London: Chatto & Windus, 1983.

Buber, M., 'Distance and Relation', *Psychiatry*, 20 (1957), pp. 97–104.

Campbell, A. V., *Rediscovering Pastoral Care*, rev. edn London: Darton, Longman and Todd, 1986.

Cantwell Smith, W., *The Meaning and End of Religion*, London: SPCK, 1978.

Cantwell Smith, W., *Faith and Belief*, Princeton University Press, 1979.

Capps, D., *Life Cycle Theory and Pastoral Care*, London: Fortress Press, 1983.

Capra, F., *The Tao of Physics*, 3rd edn, London: Harper-Collins, 1992.

Carroll, L., *Alice in Wonderland*, London: Macmillan 'Miniature Edition', 1907.

Chodorow, N., *The Reproduction of Mothering*, London: University of California Press, 1978.

Clark, K., *Civilisation: a Personal View*, London: BBC Publications, 1969.

Coleridge, S. T., *Biographia Literaria*, ed. J. Engell and W. J. Bate, London: Routledge and Kegan Paul, 1983, collected works, vol. 7: 2.

Coles, R., *The Spiritual Life of Children*, London: Harper-Collins, 1992.

Colledge, E. and Walsh, J., (trans.), *Julian of Norwich: Showings*, London: Paulist Press and SPCK, 1978.

Cracknell, K., *Towards a New Relationship*, Manchester: Epworth Press, 1986.

Cupitt, D., *Life Lines*, London: SCM Press, 1986.

Dickens, C., *Hard Times*, 1854.

Dinnerstein, D., *The Rocking of the Cradle and the Ruling of the World*, London: The Women's Press, 1987.

Dunne, J. S., *Time and Myth*, London: SCM Press, 1973.

Dunne, J. S., *The Way of All the Earth: an Encounter with Eastern Religions*, London: Sheldon Press, 1973.

Dunne, J. S., *The Reasons of the Heart*, London: SCM Press, 1978.

Eliot, G., *Middlemarch*, London: Pan Books, 1973.

Eliot, T. S., 'Four Quartets' *The Complete Poems and Plays of T. S. Eliot*, London: Faber & Faber, 1969.

Erikson, E., *Young Man Luther*, London: Faber & Faber, 1959.

Erikson, E., *Childhood and Society*, London: Penguin Books, 1965.

Erikson, E., *Identity, Youth and Crisis*, London: Faber & Faber, 1968.

Erikson, E., *Gandhi's Truth*, New York: Norton, 1969.

Erikson, E., *Toys and Reasons*, London: Marion Boyars, 1978.

Faber, H., *Psychology of Religion*, London: SCM Press, 1976.

Fingarette, H., *The Self in Transformation*, New York: Basic Books, 1963.

Ford-Grabowsky, M., 'The Fullness of the Christian Faith Experience: Dimensions Missing in Faith Development Theory', *Journal of Pastoral Care*, 61:1 (1987).

Fordham, F., *An Introduction to Jung's Psychology*, London: Penguin Books, 1966.

Forrester, J., *The Seductions of Psychoanalysis*, Cambridge University Press, 1990.

Fowler, J. W., *Stages of Faith: the Psychology of Human Development and the Quest for Meaning*, San Francisco: Harper and Row, 1981.

Fowler, J. W., *Becoming Adult, Becoming Christian*, San Francisco: Harper and Row, 1984.

Fowler, J. W., *Faith Development and Pastoral Care*, Philadelphia: Fortress Press, 1987.

Fox, M., *Meditations with Eckhart*, Santa Fe: Bear and Co., 1983.

Freud, A., *Normality and Pathology in Childhood*, London: Penguin Books, 1973.

Freud, S., *Analysis Terminable and Interminable*, standard edn, London: Hogarth Press, vol. 23.

Freud, S., *Beyond the Pleasure Principle*, London: Penguin Freud Library, vol. 11.

Freud, S., *The Dissolution of the Oedipus Complex*, London: Penguin Freud Library, vol. 7.

Freud, S., *Formulations of the Two Principles of Mental Functioning*, London: Penguin Freud Library, vol. 11.

Freud, S., *The Future of an Illusion*, London: Penguin Freud Library, vol. 12.

Freud, S., *New Introductory Lectures on Psychoanalysis*, London: Penguin Freud Library, vol. 2.

Freud, S., *Obsessive Actions and Religious Practices*, London: Penguin Freud Library, vol. 13.

Freud, S., *One of the Difficulties of Pschoanalysis*, London: Hogarth Press, 1946, collected papers, 4.

Freud, S., *An Outline of Psychoanalysis*, London: Penguin Freud Library, vol. 15.

Freud, S., *Postscript to 'The Question of Lay Analysis'*, London: Penguin Freud Library, vol. 15.

Freud, S., *Three Essays on the Theory of Sexuality*, London: Penguin Freud Library, vol. 7.

Freud, S., *Totem and Taboo*, London: Penguin Freud Library, vol. 13.

Fromm, E., *Psychoanalysis and Religion*, Yale University Press, 1967.

Fromm, E., *The Greatness and Limitations of Freud's Thought*, London: Jonathan Cape, 1980.

Gatta, J., *A Pastoral Art*, London: Darton, Longman and Todd, 1987.

Gilligan, C., *In a Different Voice: Psychological Theory and Women's Development*, Harvard University Press, 1982.

Golan, N., *Passing Through Transitions*, London: Collier Macmillan, 1981.

Goldman, R., *Religious Thinking from Childhood to Adolescence*, London: Routledge and Kegan Paul, 1964.

Goldman, R., *Readiness for Religion*, London: Routledge and Kegan Paul, 1965.

Guntrip, H., *Psychoanalytic Theory, Therapy and the Self*, London: Hogarth Press, 1971.

Harding, D. E., *On Having No Head*, London and New York: Arkana, 1986.

Hemenway, J., 'Four Faith Frameworks', *Journal of Pastoral Care*, 38:4 (1984), pp. 317–23.

Jacobs, M., 'Naming and Labelling', *Contact*, 3 (1976).

Jacobs, M., *The Presenting Past*, Buckingham: Open University Press, 1986.

Jacobs, M., *Faith or Fear?*, London: Darton, Longman and Todd, 1987.

Jacobs, M., *Towards the Fullness of Christ*, London: Darton, Longman and Todd, 1988.

Jacobs, M., 'Is anatomy destiny?' in R. Holloway (ed.) *Who Needs Feminism? Male Responses to Sexism in the Church*, London: SPCK, 1991.

Jacobs, M., *Sigmund Freud*, London: Sage Publications, 1992.

Jones, A., *Soul Making*, London: SCM Press, 1986.

Joyce, J., *A Portrait of the Artist as a Young Man*, London: Jonathan Cape, 1916.

Jung, C. G, *Psychology and Religion*, London: Routledge and Kegan Paul, 1958, collected works, vol. 11.

Jung, C. G., *Symbols of Transformation*, London: Routledge and Kegan Paul, 1966, collected works, vol. 5.

Justice, W. G. and Lambert, W., 'A Comparative Study of the Language People Use to Describe the Personalities of God and their Earthly Parents', *Journal of Pastoral Care*, 40:2 (1986), pp. 166–72.

Klein, M., *Envy and Gratitude and Other Works 1946–1963*, London: Hogarth Press, 1975.

Kohlberg, L., *The Philosophy of Moral Development*, San

Francisco: Harper and Row, 1981.

Kohlberg, L., 'Education, Moral Development and Faith', *Journal of Moral Education*, 4:1.

Leech, K., *True God*, London: Sheldon Press, 1985.

Levinson, D., *et al., The Seasons of a Man's Life*, New York: Knopf, 1978.

Lewis, C. S., *The Last Battle*, London: Penguin Books, 1964.

Loades, A., *Searching for Lost Coins: Explorations in Christianity and Feminism*, London: SPCK, 1987.

Lodge, D., *How Far Can You Go?*, London: Secker & Warburg, 1980.

Lomas, P., *True and False Experience*, London: Allen Lane, 1973.

London, J., *White Fang*, London: Macmillan, 1906.

McFague, S., *Models of God,* London: Fortress Press and SCM Press, 1987.

McGlashan, A., *Savage and Beautiful Country*, London: Chatto & Windus, 1966.

Maitland, S., *Three Times Table*, London: Virago Press, 1990.

Manley Hopkins, G., *Gerard Manley Hopkins: a Selection of His Poems and Prose*, ed. W. H. Gardner, London: Penguin Books, 1953.

Mascaró, J., *The Upanishads*, London: Penguin Books, 1965.

Ministry to the Sick, *Authorized Alternative Services*, London: SPCK, 1983.

Mosley, N., *Hopeful Monsters*, London: Secker & Warburg, 1990.

Mott, M., *The Seven Mountains of Thomas Merton*, London: Sheldon Press, 1986.

Muuss, R., *Theories of Adolescence*, 2nd edn, New York: Random House, 1968.

Page, F. (ed.), *The Letters of John Keats*, Oxford University Press, 1954.

Palmer, H., *The Enneagram: Understanding Yourself and Others in Your Life*, London: HarperCollins, 1991.

Phillips, J. L., *The Origins of Intellect*, New York: W. H. Freeman, 1975.

Pruyser, P. W., *The Play of the Imagination: Toward a Psychoanalysis of Culture*, New York: International Universities Press, 1983.

Rayner, E., *Human Development*, 2nd edn, London: Allen & Unwin, 1978.

Reed, B., *The Dynamics of Religion*, London: Darton, Longman and Todd, 1978.

Renner, H. P. V., 'The Use of Ritual in Pastoral Care', *Journal of Pastoral Care*, 33:3 (1979), pp. 164–74.

Religious Society of Friends, The, *Questions and Counsel*, 1988.

Riso, O., *Practical Guide to Personality Types: Understanding the Enneagram*, London: Aquarian Press, 1988.

Rizzuto, A.-M., *The Birth of the Living God*, University of Chicago Press, 1979.

Robinson, J., *Honest to God*, London: SCM Press, 1963.

Rogers, C., *Freedom to Learn*, Ohio: Merrill, 1969.

Roudinesco, E., *Jacques Lacan and Co.*, London: Free Association Books, 1990.

Samuels, A., *Jung and the Post-Jungians*, London: Routledge and Kegan Paul, 1985.

Schmidt, W. S., 'An Ontological Model of Development', *Journal of Pastoral Care*, 40:1 (1986), pp. 56–67.

Searles, H., *The Nonhuman Environment in Normal Development and in Schizophrenia*, New York: International Universities Press, 1960.

Shah, I., *The Way of the Sufi*, London: Penguin Books, 1974.

Shakespeare, W., *The Tempest*.

Snow, C. P., *The Two Cultures and the Scientific Revolution*, Cambridge University Press, 1959, Rede Lecture.

Society of Friends, The, *Advices and Queries*, 1964.

Speck, P. and Ainsworth-Smith, I., *Letting Go: Caring for the Dying and Bereaved*, London: SPCK, 1982.

Storr, A., *Solitude*, London: Flamingo (Fontana), 1989.

Thomas, D., *Collected Poems 1934–1953*, ed, W. Davies and R. Maud, London: Dent, 1988.

Thwaite, A., *Portion for Foxes*, Oxford University Press, 1977.

Tillich, P., *The Courage to Be*, New York: Nisbet, 1952.

Tillich, P., *Dynamics of Faith*, New York: Harper, 1957.

Tolkein, J. R. R., *Tree and Leaf*, London: Unwin Books, 1964.

Turquet, P., 'Threats to Identity in the Large Group', in L. Kreeger (ed.), *The Large Group: Dynamics and Therapy*,

London: Constable, 1975.

van Belzen, J., 'The Rise of Dutch Psychology of Religion', *Changes*, 10:3 (1992).

Vergote, A., *The Religious Man*, Dublin: Gill and Macmillan, 1969.

Watts, A., *The Spirit of Zen*, London: HarperCollins, 1991.

Wilber, K., *Up from Eden: a Transpersonal View of Human Evolution*, New York: Anchor Press/Doubleday, 1981.

Wilson, A. N., *Against Religion*, Counterblast 19, London: Chatto & Windus, 1991.

Winnicott, D. W., *The Maturational Processes and the Facilitating Environment*, London: Hogarth Press, 1965.

Winnicott, D. W., *Playing and Reality*, London: Penguin Books, 1974.

Winnicott, D. W., *Collected Papers: Through Paediatrics to Psycho-analysis*, London: Hogarth Press, 1975.

Winnicott, D. W., *Home is Where We Start From*, London: Penguin Books, 1986.

Winnicott, D. W., *Human Nature*, London: Free Association Books, 1988.

Winterson, J., *Oranges are Not the Only Fruit*, London: Bloomsbury Publishing, 1991.

Wood, J., 'Chant of the Mystic Musician', *Guardian*, 20 July 1992.

Wordsworth, W., *The Poetical Works of William Wordsworth*, ed. E. de Selencourt, Oxford University Press, 1940, vol. 1.

Zaehner, R. C., *Hinduism*, Oxford University Press, 1962.

Zohar, D., *The Quantum Self*, London: HarperCollins, 1991.

Index

197